Created *to be* God's Friend Workbook

CREATED *to be* GOD'S FRIEND WORKBOOK

HENRY T. BLACKABY
& KERRY L. SKINNER

THOMAS NELSON
Since 1798

NASHVILLE DALLAS MEXICO CITY RIO DE JANEIRO

Published in Nashville, Tennessee, by Thomas Nelson. Thomas Nelson is a registered trademark of Thomas Nelson, Inc.

Thomas Nelson, Inc., titles may be purchased in bulk for educational, business, fund-raising, or sales promotional use. For information, please e-mail SpecialMarkets@ThomasNelson.com.

ISBN: 978-0-7852-6391-3

Printed in the United States of America

03 04 05 06 07 VG 6 5 4 3 2 1

Contents

Introduction vii

Unit 1: Chosen in Eternity 1

Unit 2: God's Fullness of Time 19

Unit 3: Encountered by God 35

Unit 4: A Renewal and Establishing of God's "Call" 51

Unit 5: Abram—Shaped by God 73

Unit 6: The Cost of a New Name 89

Unit 7: Wrong Counsel Brings Tragic Consequences 103

Unit 8: A Fresh Encounter with God 117

Unit 9: Faith Through Difficulties 133

Unit 10: God Entrusts Isaac to Two Prepared Parents 149

Unit 11: The Moment of Truth 165

Unit 12: Abraham—Concluding Chapter 193

Appendix 207

Notes 211

About the Authors 213

Introduction

This modest work first had its "birth" in a series of Bible studies presented to a pastor and staff annual Bible conference in California a couple of years ago. The response from those present was immediate and overwhelming. Many renewed their call into the ministry; others who were preparing to resign their ministry situations "re-signed" and went back to their churches refreshed and renewed, with a fresh touch from God—who had called them in the beginning. All of us saw our lives *from God's perspective!*

Our lives look very different when we see them from God's perspective. If we look at our lives *through* our circumstances, we will get a distorted view of God. If we "sit with Christ" (Eph. 2:4–7) and look at our lives as God sees them, and from an eternal perspective, *all is different!* Even the most difficult and bewildering (and potentially discouraging) times are then seen as vital aspects of God's purposes and activities to develop our character and our intimate relationship with Him. When we see our lives as God sees them, we are encouraged, strengthened, motivated, and at peace.

We see His purposes are eternal in dimension. He created us not for time, but for eternity. His plans for us are for good, and for "a future and a hope" (Jer. 29:11). He eternally chose us (Eph. 1:3–6) in Christ and now has strategically "called" us and is shaping us for His eternal purposes (Eph. 2:4–10). All this is designed so we will respond to Him with total love, trust, and obedience, so He can be glorified in us (John 17:10), and He can accomplish His eternal purposes in and then through us.

When a child of God comes to this dimension of understanding by *faith*, there are an immediate release and yielding of his life *totally* to Him, and inexpressible *joy* and *peace* in all of life (John 15:9–11). This intimate relationship with God (a process) is seen clearly and helpfully and thoroughly in the life of Abraham.[1] To *choose* to study under the guidance of the Spirit of God (John 14:26) and from God's perspective, how God shaped Abraham, the man God called "His friend" (James 2:23; 2 Chron. 20:7; Isa. 41:8), is to expose your life to how God is working in your life to shape you for His purposes. To know the ways of God clearly is to know how to recognize when He is working in and around your life. This alerts you to respond—knowingly. You will know what awaits you if you respond by yielding your life unconditionally to Him; and you will know clearly what you will forfeit, or miss, if you say, "No!" to God.

The Scriptures give us the clearest and safest guidance in our walk with God. But you must spend careful, thoughtful time in God's Word, with a predetermined commitment to respond positively in obedience to His workings in you. To "him who knows to do good and does not do it, to him it is sin" (James 4:17); and to "sin willfully after we have received the knowledge of the truth" is unthinkable in its consequences (Heb. 10:26–31).

This study is a modest attempt, from a pastor's heart, to walk a seeking and searching child of God through God's activity in Abram (later, God changed his name to Abraham because he was responding deeply to God's relationship with him). This study is designed to

- see Abraham's life from God's perspective.
- see Abraham's response to God, as God saw it.
- see your life in your here and now as you recognize the God of Abraham, Isaac, and Jacob working in and around your life.
- help you to respond fully and immediately to Him, and enjoy His purposes manifest in you.

I am a pastor at heart. God shaped me and used me in this way for almost thirty years. With this same God-shaped heart and life I share this study. It first passed through my own life. At the request of others I now share it in this form. I have learned that no book is ever finished. No sooner has a book been released for printing than many additional thoughts and truths come to mind. These will have to wait for another time. May you, the reader, be encouraged and helped with what is shared.

Each chapter is self-contained and can be studied for the truth it presents. This may make it easier for the reader and for small group study. Questions are provided throughout the workbook to help you process the truths. Also, at the end of the workbook in the Appendix there is a chart that I believe will be most helpful in looking at the age of Abraham, corresponding Scriptures, events in the life of Abraham, God's revealed nature to Abraham, and Abraham's character development.

Please take time to study the chart on the next page before you begin.

I offer this work with the prayer that God will be pleased to use it to instruct and encourage at least some of His children, whom He loves.

SPECIAL NOTE!

This workbook can be studied individually or in a group setting. If you study in a group, two available supplemental pieces will enhance the meeting.

1. A leader's guide will give you simple ideas to keep the study flowing.
2. A twelve-unit video, consisting of ten-minute segments will introduce and stimulate discussion for each group meeting.

God's Encounters with Abraham

There are many high and low points in a person's life. As did Abraham, you may have experienced mountaintop encounters with God. Valleys or low points can also be experienced when one disobeys God or fails to consult Him. This chart is designed to help you see the significant moments of God's shaping Abraham's journey of faith and obedience. The shaping of character involves both positive and negative moments in God's shaping of Abraham. God works both negative and positive together for good in His purposes.

Before you begin the study, become familiar with the chart. Take note of Abraham's points of personal spiritual growth as you work through the book. You may want to come back to this chart at the end of each unit and note what you learned related to this picture of God's encounters with Abraham.

At the end of the study another chart will be provided to help you review God's encounters with Abraham. You will also be given opportunity to illustrate God's encounters with you.

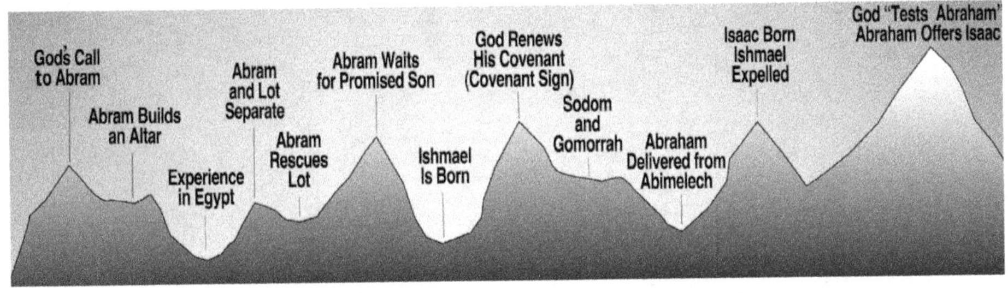

UNIT I

CHOSEN IN ETERNITY

THOUGHT STARTER

Just as He chose us in Him before the foundation of the world, that we should be holy and without blame before Him in love.

EPHESIANS 1:4

THE WAYS OF GOD ARE WONDERFUL and mysterious. Eternity is the starting point for God's activity. Paul assured the believers in Ephesus that they had been chosen "before the foundation of the world" (Eph. 1:4), having been "predestined . . . according to the good pleasure of His will" (Eph. 1:5). Paul went on to assure them of their supreme significance to God and His eternal purposes, "having made known to us the mystery of His will, according to His good pleasure which He purposed in Himself" (Eph. 1:9). This wonderful process is made clear in God's relationship with Abram.

Eternity is the starting point for God's activity.

1. God had chosen him "before the foundation of the world."
2. God called him according to the "good pleasure" of His will.
3. God "made known . . . the mystery of His will."
4. God developed him completely "according to His good pleasure."
5. And God had simply "purposed in Himself."

Each of these truths, made known clearly to us through God's call on Abram's life, is true for every believer. The process is also available to each of us. The significance of each person's life to God is every bit as real, though in the unique circumstances of each person's relationship to God.

God knew ahead of time all He would reveal to Abram. God would accomplish in and through Abram all His purposes, beginning with the call. It is, in some ways, what I experienced being born into my family. Long before I was born, I was in the hearts and planning of my parents. When I was born, it was the result of loving parents. I was sickly at birth and struggled to live. My parents did all within their love and capacity to see that I lived and grew. The struggle for life was not known to me until later in life. Not only did I live, but I also experienced so much that my parents had already purposed for me.

I lived out within my family's love all they could afford, and all I would respond to, over a lifetime of opportunity.

DAY 1

CHOSEN BY GOD

> *"And you shall be to Me a kingdom of priests and a holy nation." These are the words which you shall speak to the children of Israel.*
>
> EXODUS 19:6

God created us not for *time* but for *eternity.*

When God chooses a person for His purpose, all of eternity will be shaped by His decision.

Abram was *chosen* by God from eternity! It was in eternity that God purposed to bring salvation to a lost world through him. His plan was to do it through a nation He had formed for Himself and for this purpose. This nation would be for Him a "kingdom of priests and a holy nation" (Ex. 19:6). It would be through this nation that the Savior would come, and salvation to all people through Him. To build this nation, God purposed to begin with one man—Abram. Abram would be chosen for God's own sake. God would bring him into such an intimate relationship with Himself that all those ever after whom He would call to Himself would walk in this same relationship with God, as Abram did, and this relationship would be for all eternity. In other words, God created us not for *time* but for *eternity*.

Little did Abram know how his life would affect eternity. He had no idea that world peace and world politics would be influenced from his day even to our present day. When God chooses a person for His purpose, all of eternity will be shaped by His decision. What an awesome responsibility God gives to each person He chooses. God's choice is not for one person alone; His choice will affect people and nations for generations to come.

When did you realize that God had chosen you for a personal relationship with Him?

____

____

____

GOD'S PERSPECTIVE

One cannot understand the unfolding of God's eternal purposes in *time* without seeing the Bible from God's perspective. The Bible is the record of God. It reveals His nature and His ways in the midst of His people. It reveals the unfolding of His eternal purposes in time, especially through those He chooses and calls to Himself. His purpose in recording it in Scripture is that all those who read of the wonderful works of God would instinctively ready themselves to be encountered by God. Therefore, Genesis does not reveal Abram's walk with God (though you can read and study it for profit that way); rather, Genesis opens to our understanding the activity of God in and through a man called Abram. We cannot understand Abram's walk with God unless we see it as God saw it!

This study will seek to make clear from God's purposes and activity His relationship to Abram. This can be a God-chosen pattern for all who would walk with Him. I encourage you to apply the truths found in Abram's life to your own life. I pray you will be confronted with truth about God in such a way that you will have to make decisions in a serious response to the God of Abram in your life.

Therefore, from the very beginning you must be convinced that what God unfolds in *time* began in eternity. This truth can give every life meaning and strong purpose, and creates in you a sense of (1) purpose, (2) urgency, (3) motivation, and (4) eternal meaning.

Genesis does not reveal Abram's walk with God (though you can read and study it for profit that way); rather, Genesis opens to our understanding the activity of God in and through a man called Abram.

What priorities have you set that reveal you are responding to what God has purposed in your life?

____

____

____

What God unfolds in *time* began in eternity.

PURPOSE

To understand and believe that God did know you and chose you from eternity will give you an enormous sense of purpose. For the God of the universe to have thoughts and purposes for us also means that He will be at work in us and around us to bring them to pass. Isaiah said,

> *The LORD of hosts has sworn, saying, "Surely, as I have thought, so it shall come to pass, and as I have purposed, so it shall stand."*
>
> **ISAIAH 14:24**

Life is not meaningless; it is very purposeful. To live with purpose is to live with hope!

I can remember living out my early days of ministry in California (1957–70). Those were tumultuous days in our nation. The assassinations of President John F. Kennedy and his brother Robert, as well as Dr. Martin Luther King Jr., were the frameworks of the time. It was also a time of the intensity of the Cold War, with its sense of the immediate possibility of a nuclear war—to end all things. I saw the contrast of what God had done in my life and what was happening in many lives around me, especially the university students. I was living with a real sense of divine purpose and saw those days as purposeful and timely in the plan of God for me. God had brought me there for just such a time as this! I had purpose and meaning and urgency. I lived with a sense of excitement and anticipation—and was not disappointed. God used my life to make a difference in so many lives, and He led our churches to see just such a purpose for them.

On the other hand, those who had no relationship with God were drifting into a sense of fatalism and hopelessness. Many students dropped out of college, saying, "Why go to all the work of studying only to be blown up by a nuclear bomb?" Others began to withdraw into isolated areas and build bomb shelters. Without God, hopelessness set in. With God, intense purpose and meaning overwhelmed us. The difference was observable and enormous.

With God, intense purpose and meaning overwhelmed us. The difference was observable and enormous.

What has God purposed in your life that you are actively following in obedience to Him?

___

___

___

- **Review what God has shown you through the lesson today.**
- **Look back over your lesson and take time to underline or highlight key statements that God used to impact your life.**
- **Write a statement here that God used most in your life today:**

___

___

___

- **Turn to the end of the chapter and write your statement again. This will provide a weekly list of key statements for you to meditate on the last two days of the week.**

  ❑ CHECK THIS BOX AFTER YOU HAVE DONE SO.
- **Take time to pray, asking God to adjust your life to how He has spoken to you today.**
- **With whom do you need to share this truth today?**

___

Summary Statements

- Eternity is the starting point for God's activity.
- God created us not for time but for eternity.
- Without God, hopelessness sets in.
- For one to realize God is working out His eternal purpose in his life is to live with a sense of urgency.

DAY 2

Motivated by God

For one to realize God is working out His eternal purpose in his life is to live with a sense of urgency. Only one life to live, and it will soon be past, and only what is done with God will last. This can, if one believes this truth, bring to all of life an urgency to live meaningfully and to live well. To know God will give urgency. To have urgency will bring a willingness to obey God quickly. To know that what is done with God will last gives urgency to setting priorities and living with intentional focus and certainty not to waste life or live life carelessly.

Only one life to live, and it will soon be past, and only what is done with God will last.

In a recent conference of attorneys, many approached me—often with great emotion—affirming their deep sense of God's eternal purpose for them. Some literally trembled when this truth became real and personal to them. Out of this awareness of God's eternal activity in their lives, some had already begun entirely new ministries. Others had left the official practice of law and joined a Christian organization, like Focus on the Family, and were expressing great satisfaction. They were living their lives *from* eternity and *to* eternity! They were living intentional, purposeful, and meaningful lives that were exciting to them and their families. They had a deep sense of excitement and urgency and anticipation about their future. They seemed to desire an eternal, "Well done!" from their Lord.

How would your family and friends know that you live life with intentional focus and certainty to the point that you do not waste life or live life carelessly?

____

____

____

Paul the apostle said, "The love of Christ compels [me]" (2 Cor. 5:14). He knew God had an eternal purpose for his life. He stated emphatically, "I press on, that I may lay hold of that for which Christ Jesus has also laid hold of me . . . One thing I do . . . I press toward the goal for the prize of the upward call of God in Christ Jesus" (Phil. 3:12–14). The call of God in Paul's life was the highest motivation to give God his best. He needed no other motivation for his life.

The Amplified Bible puts this relationship between the apostle Paul and his Lord very clearly:

> *For the love of Christ controls and urges and impels us, because we are of the opinion and conviction that [if] One died for all, then all died; and He died for all, so that all those who live might live no longer to and for themselves, but to and for Him Who died and was raised again for their sake.*
>
> **2 Corinthians 5:14–15**

It was God's love and Christ's love for Paul and the world that led Him to die. Paul received that love personally. Paul's life would be nothing both in time and in eternity, had Christ not died for him. Paul saw no choice but to release his life to Jesus Christ and spend the rest of his life living for Him. Such love toward him demanded that Paul live his life in a love relationship with his Lord. Such personal love of Christ forever motivated Paul's total life. It was, to him, the only response worthy of such love.

History is full of this kind of testimony. The greater the awareness and experience of Christ's love, the deeper the motivation to serve the Lord. Jesus said, "To whom little is forgiven, the same loves little" (Luke 7:47). Jesus dramatically connected the controlling motivation of loving to forgiveness. And Paul saw himself as the chief of sinners (1 Tim. 1:15) who needed that forgiveness.

The greater the awareness and experience of Christ's love, the deeper the motivation to serve the Lord.

If Christ stood before you and asked, "What motivates your life?" what would you honestly say?

- ❑ My family
- ❑ My work
- ❑ My love for Christ
- ❑ Christ's love for me
- ❑ Friendships
- ❑ Accumulating possessions

- Review what God has shown you through the lesson today.
- Look back over your lesson and take time to underline or highlight key statements that God used to impact your life.
- Write a statement here that God used most in your life today:

____

____

____

- Turn to the end of the chapter and write your statement again. This will provide a weekly list of key statements for you to meditate on the last two days of the week.

  ❑ CHECK THIS BOX AFTER YOU HAVE DONE SO.
- Take time to pray, asking God to adjust your life to how He has spoken to you today.
- With whom do you need to share this truth today?

____

SUMMARY STATEMENTS

- Only what is done with God will last.
- To have urgency will bring a willingness to obey God quickly.
- The greater the awareness and experience of Christ's love, the deeper the motivation to serve the Lord..
- For one to realize God is working out His eternal purpose in his life is to live with a sense of urgency.

DAY 3

Eternal Meaning

Paul always lived his life with eternity in mind. Knowing that God had chosen him gave his life meaning far beyond life itself. He lived not only for time but also for eternity. He stated it this way:

> *Therefore we make it our aim, whether present or absent, to be well pleasing to Him. For we must all appear before the judgment seat of Christ, that each one may receive the things done in the body, according to what he has done, whether good or bad. Knowing, therefore, the terror of the Lord, we persuade men; but we are well known to God, and I also trust are well known in your consciences.*
>
> **2 Corinthians 5:9–11**

These factors, when real and active in a person's life, deeply affect the way he lives. Eternity is where God purposed our lives.

It is said that Billy Graham met a leading atheist in Europe one day and the man explained why he was not a Christian. He said that if he truly believed, as Christians say they believe, everyone must face eternity and give an account for how he has lived; and Jesus Christ in His death and resurrection was the only way to God and a secure eternity in heaven; and all who do not receive Christ's provision for their sin would spend eternity in a place called hell—then, he said, he would not rest day or night from warning everyone and urging everyone to respond to Christ. But, he continued, when I see the way most Christians live, I am totally convinced that what they say they believe is not true. That is why he was an atheist.

However, once this truth is appropriated into a person's life, his life will never be the same. He will never encounter life or people or circumstances without confidence in the God who chose him from eternity, and who is working out His purposes in his life now. This sense of God's eternal purpose was true of Abram, and later was true for Moses, Hannah, David, the prophets, the disciples, and the apostle Paul—and was true for every person in history greatly used of God.

This is one of the most wonderful mysteries of the Bible and should be grasped by each of God's children: God "chose us in Him [Christ] before the foundation of the world." Paul knew this profoundly and added that what God had in mind was this:

> *Just as He chose us in Him before the foundation of the world, that we should be holy and without blame before Him in love, having predestined us to adoption as sons by Jesus Christ to Himself, according to the good pleasure of His will, to the praise of the glory of His grace, by which He made us accepted in the Beloved.*
>
> **EPHESIANS 1:4–6**

How should you live if you really believe God chose you before the foundation of the world?

____

____

____

This truth can be seen throughout the entire Bible, in each of those God chooses and then uses for His eternal purposes in our world. Abram's life is a clear example of such choosing from eternity. And his response to the activity of God became forever what God would want from each, and all, of His people for all time, a walk of absolute *faith* and *obedience*.

The response to the activity of God should be a walk of absolute *faith* and *obedience.*

How is eternity affecting your life?

____

____

____

Since God has an eternal purpose for each life, it is not surprising that God, in His fullness of time, takes the initiative to come to one in whom He has chosen and reveal His purposes. In Abram's life there are two significant initiatives of God. First was while Abram was still in Ur of the Chaldeans. Stephen shared this while speaking in his defense before the high priest and the council: "Brethren and fathers, listen: The God of glory appeared to our father Abraham when he was in Mesopotamia, before he dwelt in Haran" (Acts 7:2). Later, Abram himself experienced this fact when God said to him, "I am the LORD, who brought you out of Ur of the Chaldeans, to give you this land to inherit it" (Gen. 15:7).

The second initiative of God came to him while he was in Haran. This will be dealt with at length later. However, both initiatives came from God. To our knowledge, Abram was not seeking God; God was seeking him. This is always true of God, and this is the witness of the entire Bible. It was worked out in Abram's life.

To our knowledge, Abram was not seeking God; God was seeking him.

We know little of Abram's life before God called him. But the rest of the Bible throws light on this significant moment for Abram. Several Scriptures can help us know what was on the Heart of God as He came to Abram, for example, "For the eyes of the LORD run to and fro throughout the whole earth, to show Himself strong on behalf of those whose heart is loyal to Him" (2 Chron. 16:9). And later it was said, "The LORD has sought for Himself a man after His own heart" (1 Sam. 13:14).

When God "chooses" a person for His purposes, He does so according to the person's *heart!*

When God "chooses" a person for His purposes, He does so according to the person's *heart*! The person must have a loyal heart full of trust and faith. God must have a person who loves Him "with all [the] heart, with all [the] soul, and with all [the] strength" (Deut. 6:5; Matt. 22:37). Anything less than this is unacceptable to God for the carrying out of His purposes. Unless the person had such a heart, God would find the person arguing with God, rejecting God, disobeying God, and ultimately straying from God. The eternal purposes of God could not be accomplished in such a person's life. Only a *heart* that is thoroughly loyal to Him is acceptable to God.

Do you have a heart that is loyal to Him?

❑ I DO MOST OF THE TIME. ❑ I AM MAKING ADJUSTMENTS.

❑ I NEED IMPROVEMENT. ❑ GOD IS DEALING WITH ME.

Examine how you lived life this week. How would a person know you lived by faith and obedience?

___

___

___

- **Review what God has shown you through the lesson today.**
- **Look back over your lesson and take time to underline or highlight key statements that God used to impact your life.**
- **Write a statement here that God used most in your life today:**

___

___

___

- Turn to the end of the chapter and write your statement again. This will provide a weekly list of key statements for you to meditate on the last two days of the week.

  ❑ CHECK THIS BOX AFTER YOU HAVE DONE SO.
- Take time to pray, asking God to adjust your life to how He has spoken to you today.
- With whom do you need to share this truth today?

Only a *heart* that is thoroughly loyal to Him is acceptable to God.

SUMMARY STATEMENTS

- Eternity is where God purposed our lives.
- The response to the activity of God should be a walk of absolute faith and obedience.

DAY 4

MISSED OPPORTUNITIES

Then He said to him, "I am the LORD, who brought you out of Ur of the Chaldeans, to give you this land to inherit it."

GENESIS 15:7

I have spoken with literally hundreds of people over the years whose hearts have obviously not been true to God's expectations. First, they clearly knew God was speaking to them, even calling them to Himself. Second, they struggled, often seriously, with God's right to lay claim to their lives. Excuses abounded! Arguments were raised! Resistance was evident! They were in rebellion against God! Third, all too often God withdrew, and they lost the urgent sense of His call and had only a "memory" of this experience left. Fourth, they went on doing their own will, and never knew what God could have done in them and with them.

They have been successful in helping the world achieve its goals, which last only for *time.* But it is obvious they have affected the Kingdom of God very little, if at all.

Some of these persons I have encountered years later. They have been successful in helping the world achieve its goals, which last only for *time*. But it is obvious they have affected the Kingdom of God very little, if at all. Certainly from God's eternal purposes, each person's life was wasted! Only eternity will reveal what could and should have been achieved with God.

To some I have seen God grant His mercy and come again one more time, revealing what He had intended from the beginning. These have come under grave conviction by the Holy Spirit who, in mercy, revealed to them their awful sin of resisting God. They have been broken before God, crying out to God for mercy and repenting of this awful sin of rejecting God's call earlier in their spiritual pilgrimage. God heard their cry and forgave their sin and restored them to Himself. They could never recover the years lost or the original call, but they were given another opportunity to obey His Voice, and they did. These live now with a deep sense of gratitude and urgency and focused obedience. God is using them.

I was leading a session at a national conference center and was sharing about the fear of God and the seriousness of not taking God seriously. I had stated that the loss of the fear of God creates a loss of the fear of sin. When we lose the fear of sin, we can live in rebellion against God and seemingly have no conscience about it. While I was speaking, a man ran to the front of the auditorium, fell on his knees, and began to sob, with loud cries. I spoke to him later. He said that while I was speaking, God reminded him that many years before God had called him to be an evangelist. He had rejected God's call. He said that God began to show him the many people who were in hell because he had refused God's call.

Then he cried out to me, "Is there any hope for me? Can God forgive such rebellion? Is there any hope that I could still respond, even though I know I can never recover what has now been forever lost?"

Has there been a missed opportunity in your life? Describe it.

____

____

____

If so, how did it affect your life?

____

____

____

If you missed an opportunity, how has it affected your family?

____

____

____

I assured him that there are times, in God's mercy, when delayed obedience is better than no obedience at all. He immediately pleaded for God's mercy. Soon he was at peace and assured me he knew beyond a question that God had now given him another chance. We prayed together, and he left a broken but joyful new man.

The Scriptures also indicate that it is God Himself who works on the heart to cause it to be loyal to Himself. Paul described it this way: "Work out your own salvation with fear and trembling; for it is God who works in you both to will [want to] and to do for His good pleasure" (Phil. 2:12–13).

When God encounters a person such as Abram, or when God saves a person, He has something in mind. It is not merely so the person can go to heaven when he dies. It will include this, but God has much more in mind. Paul understood that God has so much in mind when He saves a person that it ought to cause him to tremble, just to realize he is in His Presence and His unfolding purpose. Paul then urged the believers to let the fullest possible purpose of God work into every area of their lives. Let God shape your mind so you can know Him and His ways and purposes fully. Let God affect your heart and your emotions to match everything He will reveal to you of His will. Let Him affect your will so you will want to do all He reveals and do it in *faith*, believing and obeying Him.

Let God shape your mind so you can know Him and His ways and purposes fully.

Paul concluded by saying that you ought to respond to your salvation this way for two reasons:

1. It is God Himself who is at work in you causing you to want to do His will.
2. It is God who is at work in you enabling you to do all He asks of you. He will never urge you to respond to His will where He will not at the same time enable you to fully accomplish His will.

- **Review what God has shown you through the lesson today.**
- **Look back over your lesson and take time to underline or highlight key statements that God used to impact your life.**
- **Write a statement here that God used most in your life today:**

____

____

____

- **Turn to the end of the chapter and write your statement again. This will provide a weekly list of key statements for you to meditate on the last two days of the week.**

  ❑ CHECK THIS BOX AFTER YOU HAVE DONE SO.

- **Take time to pray, asking God to adjust your life to how He has spoken to you today.**
- **With whom do you need to share this truth today?**

SUMMARY STATEMENTS

- Abram was not seeking God; God was seeking him.
- When God "chooses" a person for His purposes, He does so according *to* the person's heart!
- Only a heart that is thoroughly loyal to Him is acceptable to God.
- Let God shape your mind so you can know Him and His ways and purposes fully.

DAY 5

FULFILLED OPPORTUNITIES

Years ago our family moved from a growing and dynamic church in Downey, California, to a church in Saskatoon, Saskatchewan, Canada. The move was extremely trying on my wife, Marilynn. The church we moved to had about ten people remaining as members. These last few members really wanted to disband the church. We had no money; we had no family nearby; all of our friends were gone; the weather was dramatically different; and we had four young sons and learned we were expecting another child. I was gone frequently seeking to build and strengthen this little church and to begin new mission churches. Marilynn felt so alone and helpless. She knew God had called us. In our heads we knew God would sustain and provide for our needs. But she needed a personal assurance from God that what He had asked of us, He would work out to completion in us and through us. God gave her that assurance in one simple Scripture: "I will never leave you nor forsake you" (Heb. 13:5; Deut. 31:6). That was enough! He had spoken and peace had come. The way was not easy but it was secure. Looking back over those years confirms with great joy the faithfulness of God and the timeliness of that word from God.

So thorough is God's working in the person He chooses and calls that the initiatives of God are themselves His guarantee for completion!

So thorough is God's working in the person He chooses and calls that the initiatives of God are themselves His guarantee for completion!

What He began in Abram, in His first encounter in Ur, the rest of the chapters in Genesis will reveal He completes. Remembering how God worked with Abram, what an absolute affirmation to all who would experience this in their lives. And what absolute confident expectation should rest in every life who today knows the call of God on him.

Later, Jesus sought to have His disciples understand their relationship to Him—from God's perspective also! From the very moment that Jesus called His disciples to Himself, to follow Him, He had committed Himself to love them to the end—to His last moment with them, and to the end of each one's life. What He had begun in them He would bring to completion. Even as His own life was coming to an end, it is stated: "Having loved His own who were in the world, He loved them to the end" (John 13:1).

It is so important to notice that both in Abram and in Jesus' disciples, there is no sign of "rebellion," except with Judas (John 17:12). There is sin in other areas of their lives, but one does not see an attitude of wanting to do the wrong thing. They may fail, but not out of rebellion or hardness of heart. They had to learn the hard way often, but God was present to forgive, guide, and encourage them. They always responded in loving *faith* and continued *obedience*!

Jesus wanted the disciples to realize several significant truths, which Abram would know thoroughly, as God initiated His call to them. (It is important to tie God's working with Abram and Jesus' working with His disciples in order to encourage us to see God's pattern in calling and working in our lives today.)

1. "You did not choose Me, but I chose you and appointed you" (John 15:16). In John 17 it is clear it was the Father's initiative that chose them, and He gave them to Jesus to fulfill the Father's purpose in them.

> *I have manifested Your name to the men whom You have given Me out of the world. They were Yours, You gave them to Me, and they have kept Your word. Now they have known that all things which You have given Me are from You. For I have given to them the words which You have given Me; and they have received them, and have known surely that I came forth from You; and they have believed that You sent Me.*
>
> **JOHN 17:6–8**

2. God had a purpose in choosing and calling them. That they "should go and bear fruit" (John 15:16). If they would respond to His initiatives in them daily, God Himself would accomplish great things in them and through them. They would be used of God to turn their "world upside down" (Acts 17:6). Multitudes across the world would have changed lives because of them.

3. "And that your fruit should remain" (John 15:16). Their lives, under God's control, would affect the world for the rest of time and even into eternity. Nothing God would do through them would ever be lost!

When God takes the initiative, He brings to completion all that is on His Heart.

Abram came into the full experience of such activity of God in his life! He would learn that when God takes the initiative, He brings to completion all that is on His Heart. God is not only the "beginning" or "Alpha," but also the "ending" or "Omega" (Rev. 1:11, 17). As we also have the privilege of seeing Abram's life from the beginning to the end, and then following God's activity through Abram to the end of the New Testament, we can know the truth of God's faithfulness and we can be set free to obey Him in our own lives.

Later, God assured Isaiah of this when He said,

> *Remember the former things of old,*
> *For I am God, and there is no other;*
> *I am God, and there is none like Me,*
> *Declaring the end from the beginning,*
> *And from ancient times things that are not yet done,*
> *Saying, "My counsel shall stand,*
> *And I will do all My pleasure,"*
> *Calling a bird of prey from the east,*
> *The man who executes My counsel, from a far country.*
> *Indeed I have spoken it;*
> *I will also bring it to pass.*
> *I have purposed it;*
> *I will also do it.*
>
> **ISAIAH 46:9–11**

All throughout the Bible this is one of the certain *ways* of God. He takes the initiative! And what He initiates, He completes (Phil. 1:6)!

How many times I have had individuals come to me indicating that they believed that God was "taking the initiative" in their lives. God was moving in certain and specific directions. I have turned to these Scriptures, and Biblical examples, to assure them that this is how God works. God does take the initiative! Others, however, have then begun to indicate to me what "*they* like" or what "*they* are gifted at doing" or what "*they* have always wanted to do"! I have immediately sought to assist them to seek out carefully the divine pattern of God's initiative clearly experienced through Scripture. I have encouraged them to pray. I have asked them to look carefully at their circumstances and to seek the counsel of others. I have assured them that it was indeed God who took the initiative.

Abram's response was immediate, thorough, and full of *faith*.

There is no question that God took the initiative in Abram's life. And Abram's response was immediate, thorough, and full of *faith*. He evidently knew God well enough to (1) know it was God; (2) know how important it was to obey

God; and (3) set his *heart* and life to obey God. Abram did not then recite his qualifications and gifts and his vision for serving God. He immediately obeyed God.

It is important at this moment to remind ourselves that God works and "gives light" to "every man coming into the world" (John 1:9). This means your life! Do you believe Him when He makes this important statement in John's Gospel? Are you looking for such "initiatives" of God in your life? If He were to reveal, suddenly, for you to do what He asked Abram, would you respond immediately? Are you willing, right now, to release your life to Him, in love and faith and obedience, so He can reveal His eternal purpose for your life?

Is your *heart* sufficiently responsive and committed to God that *He* knows you will respond to Him no matter what He directs?

❑ Yes, I believe it is.

❑ No.

❑ I'm not sure.

❑ I want to be responsive.

❑ I think I would respond to Him.

- **Review what God has shown you through the lesson today.**
- **Look back over your lesson and take time to underline or highlight key statements that God used to impact your life.**
- **Write a statement here that God used most in your life today:**

____

____

____

- **Turn to the end of the chapter and write your statement again. This will provide a weekly list of key statements for you to meditate on the last two days of the week.**

  ❑ Check this box after you have done so.
- **Take time to pray, asking God to adjust your life to how He has spoken to you today.**
- **With whom do you need to share this truth today?**

____

Summary Statements

- So thorough is God's working in the person He chooses and calls that the initiatives of God are themselves His guarantee for completion!
- When God takes the initiative, He brings to completion all that is on His Heart.

KEY STATEMENTS FOR MEDITATION

Day 1

Day 2

Day 3

Day 4

Day 5

UNIT 2

GOD'S FULLNESS OF TIME

Thought Starter

But when the fullness of the time had come, God sent forth His Son, born of a woman, born under the law.

Galatians 4:4

And the Scripture was fulfilled which says, "Abraham believed God, and it was accounted to him for righteousness." And he was called the friend of God.

James 2:23

Everything God does is in His "fullness of time"! This was true of creation; the Covenant with Abraham that set in motion the beginning of a nation that would be special to Him; the Exodus when He delivered the people out of bondage; and the timing of the birth of His Son. This is a pattern of God's ways, revealed in Scriptures.

If God revealed this "timing" for His activity throughout Scripture—and all of history since then has had credible witnesses to this—you can look for and expect Him to be this way in your life. This chapter will help you to understand this and respond to God's "timing" in your life also.

DAY 1

Chosen by God

"Why now? Why me? Why this?" These are phrases I hear constantly from those God is calling to Himself! Without thinking it through, we immediately resist God's right to lay claim to our lives! This is too often true even with those God eventually used significantly in the Bible. Certainly Moses is a clear example (Ex. 3–5); Jacob "wrestled" with God; and Thomas just would not believe without further evidence.

Without thinking it through, we immediately resist God's right to lay claim to our lives!

Have you ever resisted God's will? If so, explain your reason for the resistance.

____

____

____

One of my sons expressed a common reason for his resisting God's call in his life. He was a "pastor's son," and he just knew everyone expected he would follow in the steps of his father—and become a pastor. He stood and gave testimony to this fact in a worship service where he finally yielded his life fully to God's will! His full response to God encouraged and his example led several others in that same service to openly obey God's call on their lives. What a time of rejoicing we experienced!

However, even though God knows we will tend to resist Him in such a life-changing moment of His call, He is patient and kind and gentle, but never "forces" us to respond. He draws us by His love to respond.

But God is looking for the one "whose heart is loyal [complete] to Him" (2 Chron. 16:9). He found such a person in Abram! Constantly throughout the Bible the phrase "in My sight" is used. Nothing happens either good or bad on this earth that is not in God's sight. It is absolutely critical that we understand how God notices our lives. For example, God noted that His servants Moses, Jacob, and David did what was right.

Nothing happens either good or bad on this earth that is not in God's sight.

MOSES' EXAMPLE:

> *So the LORD said to Moses, "I will also do this thing that you have spoken; for you have found grace* in My sight, *and I know you by name."*
>
> **EXODUS 33:17 (emphasis added)**

JACOB'S EXAMPLE:

But now, thus says the LORD, *who created you, O Jacob,*
And He who formed you, O Israel:
"Fear not, for I have redeemed you;
I have called you by your name;
You are Mine.
When you pass through the waters, I will be with you;
And through the rivers, they shall not overflow you.
When you walk through the fire, you shall not be burned,
Nor shall the flame scorch you.
For I am the LORD *your God,*
The Holy One of Israel, your Savior;
I gave Egypt for your ransom,
Ethiopia and Seba in your place.
Since you were precious in My sight,
You have been honored,
And I have loved you;
Therefore I will give men for you,
And people for your life."

ISAIAH 43:1–4 (emphasis added)

DAVID'S EXAMPLE:

Then it shall be, if you heed all that I command you, walk in My ways, and do what is right in My sight, *to keep My statutes and My commandments, as My servant David did, then I will be with you and build for you an enduring house, as I built for David, and will give Israel to you.*

1 KINGS 11:38 (emphasis added)

On the other extreme, God very clearly noted that David had also done much that was not right:

But the word of the LORD *came to me, saying, "You have shed much blood and have made great wars; you shall not build a house for My name, because you have shed much blood on the earth* in My sight."

1 CHRONICLES 22:8 (emphasis added)

Nor did God ignore what His people had done.

> *"For the children of Judah have done evil* in My sight," *says the* LORD. *"They have set their abominations in the house which is called by* My *name, to pollute it."*
>
> **JEREMIAH 7:30 (emphasis added)**

Long before we heard His call, God had been observing carefully the growing condition of our hearts, especially our hearts toward Him. In God's "fullness of time"—when He sees that the condition of our hearts toward Him is matching His purposes in the world—He announces and reveals His purposes.

God never reveals Himself or His purposes incidentally, or accidentally, or casually! It is always in His "fullness of the time" (Gal. 4:4). And to connect this eternal truth with Abram and our lives also, we must begin with the insight to the ways of God given in Hebrews 1:1–2: "God, who at various times and in various ways spoke in time past to the fathers by the prophets, has in these last days spoken to us by His Son, whom He has appointed heir of all things, through whom also He made the worlds."

God never reveals Himself or His purposes incidentally, or accidentally, or casually!

In tomorrow's assignment we will explore this truth further.

How has God revealed Himself and His purposes to you in your most recent act of obedience?

___

___

___

- **Review what God has shown you through the lesson today.**
- **Look back over your lesson and take time to underline or highlight key statements that God used to impact your life.**
- **Write a statement here that God used most in your life today:**

___

___

___

- **Turn to the end of the chapter and write your statement again. This will provide a weekly list of key statements for you to meditate on the last two days of the week.**

  ❑ CHECK THIS BOX AFTER YOU HAVE DONE SO.
- **Take time to pray, asking God to adjust your life to how He has spoken to you today.**

- **With whom do you need to share this truth today?**

SUMMARY STATEMENTS

- Without thinking it through, we immediately resist God's right to lay claim to our lives!
- God never reveals Himself or His purposes incidentally, or accidentally, or casually!

DAY 2

THE PATTERN OF FAITH

It was in God's "fullness of time" that He sent forth His Son—and it has always been in God's "fullness of time" that He has *chosen* and *called* those He was purposing to use or work through, to accomplish His eternal purpose in the world. This was especially true of Abram. God had a crucial purpose for Abram. God was looking for a man whose walk with Him would be "perfect" (that is, complete in every way). He was looking for someone whose *faith* in Him, whose *walk* with Him, would be everything that He knew was necessary in His great plan to save sinners from their sin. It would take a certain kind of *faith* to save a person from his sin. He was looking for someone who would so *believe* Him that God could "account it to him for righteousness."

He was looking for someone who would so *believe* Him that God could "account it to him for righteousness."

Stop and take time to look up each of the following Scriptures: Genesis 15:6; Romans 4:3, 9–25; Galatians 3:6; James 2:23. After reading them, put in your own words why righteousness was credited to Abram.

God purposed that such *faith* would be the "pattern" for all who would ever put their *faith* in Him, or His Son. This was the kind of faith God was looking for, and He found it and shaped it to fullness in Abram. The life of Abram became the authentic sample of *faith* that is acceptable to God "for righteousness." We will examine this *faith* much more closely in a later chapter, for it is so fundamental to our relationship with God—in time, and in eternity!

It was God's fullness of time in His eternal purposes for Abram that God was beginning to establish a nation, special to Himself, through which He would bring a Savior. A Messiah would come through Abram and his seed. It was now God's time to begin the process that would take hundreds of years and would climax in the birth of His Son, our Lord Jesus. He would first bring Abram into an intimate relationship with Himself. He would then begin the process of shaping a man of *faith*, upon which He could build a nation. God would develop in that nation the same kind of intimate relationship of *faith* with Him that God developed in Abram. They would become a "special people," a "holy nation," a "people belonging to God," and a "kingdom of priests" (Ex. 19:3–6; 1 Peter 2:9–10). This tremendous process of intimacy with God began in God's "fullness of time," through the life of Abram, a man of *faith*.

He would first bring Abram into an intimate relationship with Himself. He would then begin the process of shaping a man of faith, upon which He could build a nation.

Think of a person in your life whom you would describe as a person of faith. Write a sentence that would describe him as a person of faith:

____

____

____

Now, write a sentence that would describe you as a person of faith:

____

____

____

- **Review what God has shown you through the lesson today.**
- **Look back over your lesson and take time to underline or highlight key statements that God used to impact your life.**
- **Write a statement here that God used most in your life today:**

____

____

____

- **Turn to the end of the chapter and write your statement again. This will provide a weekly list of key statements for you to meditate on the last two days of the week.**

  ❑ CHECK THIS BOX AFTER YOU HAVE DONE SO.
- **Take time to pray, asking God to adjust your life to how He has spoken to you today.**

- **With whom do you need to share this truth today?**

____

Summary Statements

- God is looking for a person whose walk with Him is complete in every way.
- In God's fullness of time He chooses you to accomplish His eternal purposes.

DAY 3

God's Timing and the Body

What is God *beginning* now in your life, in your family, or in your church? Is this God's "fullness of time" for you? Do you sense a stirring in your heart and life and family? The lives of others, described in the Scriptures, are *examples* for us. Paul, reviewing the life of the children of Israel, said, "Now all these things happened to them as examples, and they were written for our admonition, upon whom the ends of the ages have come" (1 Cor. 10:11).

What would you say that God is beginning in your life, in your family, or in your church? Do you sense a stirring in your heart and life and family?

____

____

____

God made me, as a pastor, aware of and alert to His "fullness of time"! Nothing was accidental. And only in immediate obedience would we later see the serious implications of that moment in time for us. So I alerted our church family to what we believed was God's perfect timing!

God made me, as a pastor, aware of and alert to His "fullness of time"! Nothing was accidental.

I received a phone call from someone whom I had never met. He began by saying, "God has clearly led me to call you." This alerted me immediately. I took his words seriously and personally. He went on to say he and his church had been traveling from North Dakota to Winnipeg, Manitoba, Canada, to lead a small group of people in a Bible study. He was told he could not do this any longer. But these dear people desperately desired to establish a church there in their city of 500,000 people.

This man said, "As I have prayed earnestly about this, God placed you and your church on my heart. Would you and your church be willing to sponsor a new mission church in Winnipeg, and minister to these people?"

What would I do? Would I reason that it was just too far a distance from our home? Would I simply reason that this man should not have started something that he could not finish? It was evident to me that my faith was being tested!

It was evident to me that my faith was being tested!

If this happened to you, how would you respond?

God knew years before this phone call that I would face this decision. Several years before that event God had led my heart to say, "Lord, if at any time, anywhere, You make me aware of a group of people who desire to have a Bible study or a church, I will respond!" At that moment of decision, I believe God was testing my heart before Him.

This city of Winnipeg was 510 miles away from our church. Our church would have to drive that distance regularly to be obedient, and usually that meant I would be the one going! This meant there would be much time, effort, finances, and other sacrifices that would have to take place for us to obey. When I shared with our church family, they responded by saying, "Pastor, you've taught us to be obedient when God invites us to join Him. We must do this!"

We did obey the Lord, and God showed me later something of His timing. The church grew, we called a pastor (by faith), and this church became the mother church for a number of other new churches that eventually formed an entire association of churches. But to me, it became very personal—and God's timing was crucial. This church became the first church one of our sons pastored after graduating from seminary. Later his brother came to be the associate pastor. When I shared in the ordination of both of those sons, I recalled the moment of a phone call from North Dakota and our response. Little did I know how important it was for me to have a heart of *faith* that would obey! It is always this way with God!

Little did I know how important it was for me to have a heart of *faith* that would obey!

Is there an area of your life in which you are having difficulty obeying God? If so, make note of it.

Describe a time when God invited you to follow Him and you obeyed and saw the mighty acts of God.

- Review what God has shown you through the lesson today.
- Look back over your lesson and take time to underline or highlight key statements that God used to impact your life.
- Write a statement here that God used most in your life today:

- Turn to the end of the chapter and write your statement again. This will provide a weekly list of key statements for you to meditate on the last two days of the week.

  ❑ CHECK THIS BOX AFTER YOU HAVE DONE SO.
- Take time to pray, asking God to adjust your life to how He has spoken to you today.
- With whom do you need to share this truth today?

SUMMARY STATEMENTS

- Nothing is accidental with God.
- Having a heart to obey God will help not only you but also others around you.

DAY 4

Biblical Examples of God's Timing

It might be helpful, at this time, to give several other examples of God's "fullness of time" in the lives of specially chosen people. When God came to Moses, God had already "heard the cry" of His people, and had "come down to deliver them . . . and to bring them up . . . to a good and large land" (Ex. 3:7–8). It was God's "fullness of time" to act decisively on behalf of His people. Therefore, He came to Moses, specially chosen by God, "Come now, therefore, and I will send you to Pharaoh that you may bring My people, the children of Israel, out of Egypt" (Ex. 3:10). It was God's "fullness of time" for His eternal purposes and was therefore His "fullness of time" for Moses. Also, later, when God was ready to send a clear message to His people in the northern kingdom, He gave them warning of impending judgment, and He moved in the life of Amos to bring this message. Here is how Amos saw this moment:

It was God's "fullness of time" to act decisively on behalf of His people.

I was no prophet,
Nor was I a son of a prophet,
But I was a sheepbreeder
And a tender of sycamore fruit.
Then the LORD took me as I followed the flock,
And the LORD said to me,
"Go, prophesy to My people Israel."

Amos 7:14–15

This same pattern—God's "fullness of time"—came to the Apostle Paul (at the time called Saul). Here is how Paul described that moment in his life:

While thus occupied, as I journeyed to Damascus with authority and commission from the chief priests, at midday, O king, along the road I saw a light from heaven, brighter than the sun, shining around me and those who journeyed with me. And when we all had fallen to the ground, I heard a voice speaking to me and saying in the Hebrew language, "Saul, Saul, why are you persecuting Me? It is hard for you to kick against the goads." So I said, "Who are You, Lord?" And He said, "I am Jesus, whom you are persecuting. But rise and stand on your feet; for I have appeared to you for this purpose, to make you a minister and a witness both of the things which you have seen and of the things which I will yet reveal to you. I will deliver you from the Jewish people, as well as from the Gentiles, to whom I now send you, to open their eyes, in order to turn them from darkness to light, and from the power of Satan to God, that they may receive forgiveness of sins and an inheritance among those who are sanctified by faith in Me." Therefore, King Agrippa, I was not disobedient to the heavenly vision, but declared first to those in Damascus and in Jerusalem, and throughout all the region of Judea, and then to the Gentiles, that they should repent, turn to God, and do works befitting repentance.

ACTS 26:12–20

It was God's "fullness of time" for the Gentiles. So He came to Paul, right on schedule, and Paul said he "was not disobedient to the heavenly vision."

Can you think of other Biblical examples of God's timing? List them here:

____

____

____

Now God comes to our lives, in the midst of His "fullness of time." At such a moment as this, He looks for someone whose heart is "perfect" toward Him (2 Chron. 16:9). Could this time in history be *your* time in God's eternal purpose?

God comes to our lives, in the midst of His "fullness of time."

- **Review what God has shown you through the lesson today.**
- **Look back over your lesson and take time to underline or highlight key statements that God used to impact your life.**
- **Write a statement here that God used most in your life today:**

____

____

____

- **Turn to the end of the chapter and write your statement again. This will provide a weekly list of key statements for you to meditate on the last two days of the week.**

  ❑ CHECK THIS BOX AFTER YOU HAVE DONE SO.
- **Take time to pray, asking God to adjust your life to how He has spoken to you today.**

- **With whom do you need to share this truth today?**

____

SUMMARY STATEMENTS

- God acts decisively in your life not only for you but also for His people's sake.
- It is critical that our hearts be "perfect" toward Him so that He can use us at any given moment.

DAY 5

GOD'S TIMING MADE PERSONAL

I faced such a moment as this in my own life. Though I was an English major in university, for a number of reasons, I refused to write with the idea of publishing. I would send reports on the mighty movement of God where I was serving, but I would not write. Then I found myself in a National Lay Renewal Conference as a speaker. A godly retired businessman was leading us in a morning devotional time. Suddenly, he said, "I want each of you to go alone with God and ask God if there is anything He has been wanting you to do that you have not yet done!"

What about you? "Is there anything God has been wanting you to do that you have not yet done"?

____

____

____

"O Lord, my Lord, if You clearly, unmistakably, undeniably are showing me that I should write, I promise I will respond immediately!"

I always respond sincerely to such requests when I am in a group setting, so I knelt down before God and began to pray. The only thing that came to mind was *writing*! I thought, *No one has asked me to write, so I am* safe!

Then our leader said, "Now that God has surfaced a matter in your life, will you tell Him now that you will immediately be obedient to Him?"

I still felt *safe* and prayed, "O Lord, my Lord, if You clearly, unmistakably, undeniably are showing me that I should write, I promise I will respond immediately!"

The very next day, a key leader heard my speech, "Knowing and Doing the Will of God." He approached me by asking, "Henry, could you tell me clearly how you know the will of God?"

I said, "If you have time, I would be glad to!"

We spent all afternoon sharing. When I had finished, he said, "Henry, I have never heard the will of God shared this way. God's people must hear this. There is a great hunger to experience God and His will in the hearts of God's people. Would you be willing to put this into a course so that God's people could study it?"

This man was responsible for adult discipleship for our churches. I replied (a little uneasily), "Do you clearly, unmistakably, undeniably feel I should write this?"

His reply was firm: "I am convinced of God you should write this and I will help you."

My reply was, "You've caught me at a most significant time. Only yesterday did I make a solemn commitment to write if God should clearly show me that I should. I don't have an option. I will do it immediately. But," I added quickly, "I've never written, so I do not know what to do."

He said, "I'll put an editor with you who will help you in putting this together." Thus began the writing of *Experiencing God: Knowing and Doing the Will of God.*[1] We then, knowing God was working in His time, asked about thirty people to pray for us while we wrote. Their assignment was to pray that God would help us write this in such a way that it would not be just another Bible study, but that it would—in the studying of it—be an experience with God. They prayed and we wrote.

I can say that a comment I hear most from those who have studied *Experiencing God* is, "I thought this was just another Bible study. But it has been the deepest experience with God in my life! Thank you. I desperately needed this study. God has dramatically changed my life through this study."

God's "fullness of time"—both lived out and experienced in my own life! Many have confirmed that this study came at a time when God's people were searching for something that would help them go beyond what they were living in their walk with God. They wanted and were looking for two things: (1) How can Christ be more real and personal in my life? and (2) How can I clearly know and do the will of God?

I have clearly come to know this experience was indeed in the fullness of God's time. The workbook is nearing three million copies and it is in about forty-three languages. It is still in great demand after several years.

This has alerted me to other moments of God's activity and I am aware especially of God's timing!

God will be honored and many people will be greatly blessed through your faithful and obedient walk with God.

The rest of this book will help you to understand this entire experience with God for your life, as you see it unfolding in God's activity in and through the life of Abram. It will encourage you to live a life of *faith* and immediate *obedience*. God will be honored and many people will be greatly blessed through your faithful and obedient walk with God.

What about God's "fullness of time" in your life? Are you expecting it? Are you recognizing His invitations in your life? Do you need to go alone with God and ask Him if there is anything He has been asking of you? And do you need to listen and make a firm and immediate commitment to obey Him—by faith? And will you then get up from that sacred moment and watch to see what He will do next to let you know what He is asking of you? Write a prayer to God as you respond to these questions.

- **Review what God has shown you through the lesson today.**
- **Look back over your lesson and take time to underline or highlight key statements that God used to impact your life.**
- **Write a statement here that God used most in your life today:**

- **Turn to the end of the chapter and write your statement again. This will provide a weekly list of key statements for you to meditate on the last two days of the week.**

  ❑ CHECK THIS BOX AFTER YOU HAVE DONE SO.
- **Take time to pray, asking God to adjust your life to how He has spoken to you today.**
- **With whom do you need to share this truth today?**

Summary Statements

- God desires a heart that says, "Lord, whatever You ask, my answer is yes!"
- God will be honored and many people will be greatly blessed through your faithful and obedient walk with God.

KEY STATEMENTS FOR MEDITATION

Day 1

Day 2

Day 3

Day 4

Day 5

UNIT 3

ENCOUNTERED BY GOD

Thought Starter

Now the Lord *had said to Abram: "Get out of your country, from your family and from your father's house, to a land that I will show you. I will make you a great nation; I will bless you and make your name great; and you shall be a blessing. I will bless those who bless you, and I will curse him who curses you; and in you all the families of the earth shall be blessed." So Abram departed as the* Lord *had spoken to him, and Lot went with him. And Abram was seventy-five years old when he departed from Haran.*

Genesis 12:1–4

There is no more crucial moment in a person's life than when he is encountered by God! That moment sets in motion the rest of his life. Jesus gave a lasting picture of this when He spoke of the Good Shepherd: "He calls his own sheep by name and leads them out . . . He goes before them; and the sheep follow him, for they know his voice" (John 10:3–4).

There is no more crucial moment in a person's life than when he is encountered by God!

This is exactly what was happening in the life of Abram. First, God was the Good Shepherd, and He took the initiative to call Abram by name and lead him out. Second, Abram knew God's Voice and followed Him with great *faith* and trust and confidence. The true Shepherd is Himself the door who opens to His sheep—in His timing, in His way, and for His purposes.

Psalm 23 gives us an even clearer and more simple picture of the Shepherd and His sheep. This will be seen and experienced in the life of Abram and will become a wonderful eternal pattern for all to see and to follow.

> *The* Lord *is my shepherd; I shall not want. He makes me to lie down in green pastures; He leads me beside the still waters. He restores my soul; He leads me in the paths of righteousness for His name's sake. Yea, though I walk through the valley of the shadow of death, I will fear no evil; for You are with me; Your rod and Your staff, they comfort me. You prepare a table before me in the presence of my enemies; You anoint my head with oil; my cup runs over. Surely goodness and mercy shall follow me all the days of my life; and I will dwell in the house of the* Lord *forever.*
>
> Psalm 23:1–6

Every encounter by God in an individual's life has this very potential! Though expressed uniquely in each person, the fullness of life provided by God is the same. Take time to meditate on Psalm 23 before you continue reading this book! Meet God in His Shepherd's Heart, before you proceed. Release your life to Him and ask Him to now guide you, as He did Abram. Begin to see your life as God sees it!

DAY 1

God Encounters Abram

And Terah took his son Abram and his grandson Lot, the son of Haran, and his daughter-in-law Sarai, his son Abram's wife, and they went out with them from Ur of the Chaldeans to go to the land of Canaan; and they came to Haran and dwelt there. So the days of Terah were two hundred and five years, and Terah died in Haran.

Genesis 11:31–32

Though Genesis 11:31 says, "And Terah took his son Abram . . . and they went out . . . from Ur . . . to go to the land of Canaan; and they came to Haran and dwelt there," the Scriptures also indicate clearly that it was Abram whom God came to and directed to leave Ur and go to a land that God would show him. God's purpose was with Abram. In Acts 7:2–3, Stephen affirmed:

> *Brethren and fathers, listen: The God of glory appeared to our father Abraham when he was in Mesopotamia, before he dwelt in Haran, and said to him, "Get out of your country and from your relatives, and come to a land that I will show you."*

Later in Genesis 15:7, God Himself spoke to Abram and reminded him: "I am the LORD, who brought you out of Ur of the Chaldeans, to give you this land to inherit it." There are several wonderful and far-reaching features about this moment of first encounter with God.

Features of an Encounter with God:

1. God takes the initiative to reveal His will.

God always takes the initiative when He is about to accomplish His purposes through the one He chooses.

First, God took the initiative to come to Abram. He came to reveal His will to him. Like a Good Shepherd, He was leading him out and was going before him. God always takes the initiative when He is about to accomplish His purposes through the one He chooses.

This initiative may come early in life as it did to Samuel when he was a very young boy serving Eli the priest (1 Sam. 3). God had an enormous purpose for young Samuel. At a very crucial moment in God's purposes for

Israel, Samuel would become both a prophet and a great deliverer of God's people.

God's initiative touched others even when they were perhaps teenagers, like Joseph and Daniel. His initiative could touch a maturing adult, like many of the prophets, the disciples of Jesus, or the Apostle Paul. But God's initiative can come also to senior adults, such as Elizabeth and Zacharias (Luke 1:5–8). Abram was older as well. At his second encounter, when God made a Covenant with him, he was seventy-five years old (Gen. 12:4). At any time, in any place, and in any way, God can take the initiative and encounter the one He has chosen for His purposes!

At any time, in any place, and in any way, God can take the initiative and encounter the one He has chosen for His purposes!

History is full of the testimonies of such initiatives of God. All those God uses mightily have described God's initiative in their call to serve Him. I was seventeen years old, a high-school student attending a youth rally, when suddenly I knew I was face-to-Face with God. He was making His rightful claim on my life. I felt as though no one else was present, only God and me. I did know an opportunity to respond to God's right to my life was given, and I was compelled by the strong hand of God to acknowledge God's call. That was the time I surrendered to His call. Others responded also. Some of them still speak to me with great tenderness about that moment. Since that encounter of God's initiative I have never been the same. I have never looked back. I have never struggled with any other direction for my life. God settled at that moment the direction for the rest of my life—I was His and His alone!

God settled at that moment the direction for the rest of my life—I was His and His alone!

Like Abram, I "went out, not knowing" anything of God's particulars. I only knew conclusively I was His and He was mine as Lord of all. Questioning the relationship has never been an issue. He has revealed His direction for my life one day at a time. Like Abram, I can now look back and see how God's Hand and Presence faithfully guided, protected, and provided for me. God's pattern and purpose are much clearer today than ever before. Each step with God was a huge moment of *faith*, and continues to be so to this very day.

God desired that kind of *faith* from Abram with His working in Abram's life. God had convinced him that He would be consistently the One who would best work through him to fulfill His eternal purposes. Each day would continue to be a walk of *faith*—"from faith to faith" (Rom. 1:17).

We know little of Abram's background. But we do know that he had already gained a "name" among his own family that he could be trusted. Especially was this true about his integrity with God. It is clear that Abram knew it was God, knew what He was saying, and had a heart to obey. He had been living this way for some time, and there was no hint that his immediate family did not believe him. He had made the decision to leave everything and go to a place only God knew:

It is clear that Abram knew it was God, knew what He was saying, and had a heart to obey.

> *By faith Abraham obeyed when he was called to go out to the place which he would receive as an inheritance. And he went out, not knowing where he was going.*
>
> HEBREWS 11:8

He was confident that God would let him know one day at a time. Abram simply obeyed! Even his father went with him, having to leave behind even more than Abram. No wonder God chose Abram. God knew his heart. He knew that Abram *would obey* and would begin a journey of *faith.* This journey would match all God was looking for in one upon whom He would build a nation for Himself.

When did God first encounter your life?

____

____

____

What is the last great encounter God has brought to your life?

____

____

____

- **Review what God has shown you through the lesson today.**
- **Look back over your lesson and take time to underline or highlight key statements that God used to impact your life.**
- **Write a statement here that God used most in your life today:**

____

____

____

- **Turn to the end of the chapter and write your statement again. This will provide a weekly list of key statements for you to meditate on the last two days of the week.**

  ❑ CHECK THIS BOX AFTER YOU HAVE DONE SO.
- **Take time to pray, asking God to adjust your life to how He has spoken to you today.**
- **With whom do you need to share this truth today?**

____

Summary Statements

- God always takes the initiative when He is about to accomplish His purposes through the one He chooses.
- When God encounters you, He sets the direction for the rest of your life—you are His and His alone!

DAY 2

Faith

A second feature of Abram's encounter with God is so significant, especially from God's perspective—*faith*! The nature and quality of this *faith* are the essence of God's relationship to the one He chooses. The *faith* God is looking for, first, is a certain quality of relationship with Him! This *faith* must have a heart like His. This is revealed when God said why He had chosen David and rejected Saul. Samuel told Saul: "The LORD has sought for Himself a man after His own heart" (1 Sam. 13:14).

The nature and quality of this *faith* are the essence of God's relationship to the one He chooses.

Features of an Encounter with God:

1. God takes the initiative to reveal His will.
2. **God looks for a quality of relationship toward Him that will respond in *faith*!**

The Heart of God and the heart of the one God chooses must beat as one!

The Heart of God and the heart of the one God chooses must beat as one! What is on the Heart of God must be able to be not only revealed but also received. Only a heart like God's will do both. The Scripture states, "The LORD does not see as man sees; for man looks at the outward appearance, but the LORD looks at the heart" (1 Sam. 16:7).

He looks for a quality of relationship toward Him that will respond in *faith*! *Faith*, then, is a quality of response to God that is expressed in trust, reliance, commitment, and obedience. It is an unquestioned obedience, based on who He is and the person's experience of God as He is!

Faith is an unquestioned obedience, based on who He is and the person's experience of God as He is!

Faith is based on what we know of God as He has made Himself known and as we have experienced Him! The more we simply respond to Him openly and confidently, the more He reveals of Himself. The more He reveals, the more we can trust and respond. Therefore, a growing *faith* is when God systematically reveals Himself and we believe Him and respond to Him.

What is your faith like? (Check all that apply.)

❑ SPORADIC ❑ ALWAYS OBEDIENT
❑ GROWING ❑ CONSISTENT
❑ SIMPLE ❑ COMPLEX

Faith the size of a "mustard seed" (Matt. 17:20) is all God is initially looking for. But it has to be considered *faith* from God's perspective, not from your perspective. Jesus assured His disciples that if anyone had such *faith*, "nothing will be impossible for you." Then God develops that *faith*! Strong, growing, God-sized *faith* begins with a simple step of obedience based on all we know of God. Nothing can proceed without the first step. This is the step Abram took, and God began to fulfill His eternal purpose through Abram. This is where it always begins. And this is where many fail, and never know what God could have done through their lives. They just could not take the first step of *faith* when God encountered them.

Strong, growing, God-sized *faith* begins with a simple step of obedience based on all we know of God.

Does God see in you a quality of faith represented by your trust in Him? How would people know that you have this?

____

____

____

Are you willing to take the first step, not knowing what will happen when you do? Explain how you know whether you would or not.

____

____

____

Peter obeyed, just like Abram, when Jesus asked him to leave everything and follow Him—and Christians know of Peter to this day! Many now realize the awesome things God had purposed to accomplish through Peter. It began the day Peter encountered Jesus by his fishing boat (Luke 5:1–11). He had to believe Jesus and obey Him by *faith*.

But I have met literally hundreds of grieving Christians who remember a moment in their lives when God asked them to leave everything and go where He would show them, but they just could not do it then. They have ever since prayed, cried, sought God—but have never had a return of this call in their lives. They live devoted lives to this day—but they know their lives are not what God originally purposed. That moment was lost forever! When God takes the initiative to come to us, as He did to Abram, and tell us what He wants us to do, that *is* His "fullness of time." *Obedience*, based on *faith* already established, is crucial!

***Obedience,* based on *faith* already established, is crucial!**

- **Review what God has shown you through the lesson today.**
- **Look back over your lesson and take time to underline or highlight key statements that God used to impact your life.**
- **Write a statement here that God used most in your life today:**

____

____

____

- **Turn to the end of the chapter and write your statement again. This will provide a weekly list of key statements for you to meditate on the last two days of the week.**

  ❑ CHECK THIS BOX AFTER YOU HAVE DONE SO.
- **Take time to pray, asking God to adjust your life to how He has spoken to you today.**
- **With whom do you need to share this truth today?**

____

SUMMARY STATEMENTS

- The Heart of God and the heart of the one God chooses must beat as one.
- Strong, growing, God-sized faith begins with a simple step of obedience based on all we know of God.
- Obedience, based on faith already established, is crucial!

DAY 3

Abram's Response

A third feature of Abram's first encounter with God is Abram's response. Abram responded both on what he knew of God and on what he did not know of God. A response of *faith* is based on *fact*—that is, what we *know, not on what we do not know. Faith* is never blind! *Faith* is based on the God we *know*! There may be so much more that we are going to know in the future, but the first step of *faith* upon which God moves is based on all we do know. It is evident that Abram knew enough of God to know He could be absolutely trusted, especially with something as large as this. So he obeyed God, and God took him to the next step of *faith*.

Faith* is based on the God we *know!

Features of an Encounter with God:

1. God takes the initiative to reveal His will.
2. God looks for a quality of relationship toward Him that will respond in *faith!*
3. **The *first* step of *faith* should be based on what we know about God!**

What a person does when encountered by God reveals what he believes about God! We really do not need to know all about Abram's past. When we see his immediate response to God, we know at least something about his relationship with God. We know Abram's relationship with God was based on *faith*. He knew enough of God in an intimate way to trust Him and obey Him. To our limited knowledge, we know little of the *faith* in God being expressed in the people of his day. We know only of Abram. And it is obvious his response to God was not lived out in a one-time casual experience with God. He must have had a long-standing, intimate relationship with God to make such a huge decision to move from his home in Ur and go to Haran. This decision could not have been made so quickly, thoroughly, and obediently if there were not a deep relationship between God and Abram. *God* knew *Abram's* heart, and He knew that Abram's *faith* was sufficient in character to respond. He also knew that Abram would continue to respond as God revealed His will one day at a time.

Abram was to live "from faith to faith" (Rom. 1:17). God was about to teach Abram that "the just shall live by faith" (Rom. 1:17).

A PERSONAL ENCOUNTER

I had to take the first step of obedience in writing *Experiencing God.* God *then* could develop my life—as a writer of other books also. Little did I know what God had in mind (and I still do not know what else He has in mind). I did the *first* thing He asked, and He began then to bring into my life the larger purposes that He had in mind. I could not take a second step of *faith* until I had taken the first step. The first step of *faith* would depend on the quality of that *faith.* God knew this and now I know this!

Don't let the unknown of the second step determine whether or not you will take the first step. Some people are not willing to take the first step unless they know what will happen when they do! *Faith* leaves the next step to God and "steps out" in *obedience*, believing God will supply "all things that pertain to life and godliness, through the knowledge of Him who called us by glory and virtue" (2 Peter 1:3).

Don't let the unknown of the second step determine whether or not you will take the first step.

You may be at the first step of *faith-obedience*! What you do next will reveal what you now believe about God! God will not develop your walk with Him or unfold His eternal purposes for your life—until you take that *first* step of *faith.* Remember, what may *seem* impossible to you is not impossible with God. For with God nothing is impossible (Luke 1:37; 18:27)! Then God builds on what you *know* of Him and how you respond to Him. Your first step of *faith* reveals what you know of Him. Do you want to know more of Him, in real-life experiences? Do right now what God is asking! Trust Him to bring it to pass!

Remember, what may *seem* impossible to you is not impossible with God.

Your first step of *faith* reveals what you know of Him.

What is God asking you to do that you have resisted? What is the next step of obedience that God is asking of you?

___

___

___

- **Review what God has shown you through the lesson today.**
- **Look back over your lesson and take time to underline or highlight key statements that God used to impact your life.**
- **Write a statement here that God used most in your life today:**

___

___

___

- **Turn to the end of the chapter and write your statement again. This will provide a weekly list of key statements for you to meditate on the last two days of the week.**

  ❑ CHECK THIS BOX AFTER YOU HAVE DONE SO.
- **Take time to pray, asking God to adjust your life to how He has spoken to you today.**
- **With whom do you need to share this truth today?**

SUMMARY STATEMENTS

- Faith is based on the God we know!
- Don't let the unknown of the second step determine whether or not you will take the first step.
- Remember, what may seem impossible to you is not impossible with God.
- Your first step of faith reveals what you know of Him.

DAY 4

FAITH AFFECTS OTHERS

God is not unaware of our influence on others, even though we may not have that same awareness!

There is a fourth factor that surfaces in Abram's initial encounter with God. Abram's step of *faith* and *obedience* for his own life deeply affected the lives of others around him. This was especially true of his immediate family. His family—father and other family members, their wives and children, along with trusted servants—became caught up and influenced by Abram's decision to walk by *faith* in *obedience* to God's encounter with him. If we read between the lines (which can be done if not violating all we do know from Scriptures), Abram had a very strong and persuasive *faith*. He was a leader of others. He seems to have been the pacesetter. God is not unaware of our influence on others, even though we may not have that same awareness!

FEATURES OF AN ENCOUNTER WITH GOD:

1. God takes the initiative to reveal His will.
2. God looks for a quality of relationship toward Him that will respond in faith!
3. The first step of faith should be based on what we know about God!
4. **Your step of faith and obedience will deeply affect the lives of others around you.**

These changes and influences were not minor—but major! Abram's *obedience* affected many things including himself and the others with him. Remember that your first step of *faith* will deeply affect those around you. Abram's *obedience* brought with it (1) leaving the familiar where he had lived for some time, including business, friends, comfort, security, successes, etc.; (2) having his family leave what was familiar to them, also; (3) experiencing the inconvenience of travel "into the unknown," and unfamiliar and uncertain (to them, but not to God); and (4) establishing a new place of residence, not knowing where that would be until God told him to stop. Only pure *faith* in God would take such a step. This would require of the family not only a trust in Abram, but also a trust in the God of Abram that they had observed in Abram's life.

How has your obedience to God affected the people around you?

____

____

____

Have you traveled this narrow path of *obedience* in your life? Jesus said prophetically, "There are few who find it" (Matt. 7:14). Having served as a pastor for almost thirty years, I noticed how God carefully selected the first member of a family whom He saved. That person had such a confident relation to God. The family began immediately to be greatly influenced as well. But the quality of *faith* shown in the first family member who was saved was similar to that of Abram.

ONE LIFE AFFECTS MANY

A girl with a Catholic background was saved in our church in Saskatoon, Saskatchewan, Canada. It was not long before her sister also came to know the Lord. Since then other family members have been brought into an intimate relation to Christ. Like Abram, she has gone on in her *faith*. She married a fellow college student, and both have responded to God's call into ministry. They served as pastor and wife for some time and then went to seminary. After that they directed work in an entire province and now hold a leadership role in the reaching of an entire nation. Her sister married a pastor, and they have since gone on to lead a significant institution, affecting a nation and a world. Now, other family members have joined them in God's work!

Yet not all take such a deep step of *faith*! Others may be encountered by God, encouraged by God, and maybe with equal or greater possibilities, but never respond in *faith* and *obedience*! They may not know until eternity what could have been if they had only believed and obeyed.

They may not know until eternity what could have been if they had only believed and obeyed.

- **Review what God has shown you through the lesson today.**
- **Look back over your lesson and take time to underline or highlight key statements that God used to impact your life.**
- **Write a statement here that God used most in your life today:**

____

____

____

- **Turn to the end of the chapter and write your statement again. This will provide a weekly list of key statements for you to meditate on the last two days of the week.**

  ❑ CHECK THIS BOX AFTER YOU HAVE DONE SO.
- **Take time to pray, asking God to adjust your life to how He has spoken to you today.**
- **With whom do you need to share this truth today?**

____

SUMMARY STATEMENTS

- God is not unaware of our influence on others, even though we may not have that same awareness!
- Your step of faith and obedience will deeply affect the lives of others around you.
- You may not know until eternity what could have been if you had only believed and obeyed.
- Your first step of faith reveals what you know of Him.

DAY 5

Genuine Trust

At the very beginning of Abram's *obedience* there is clear evidence of genuine trust in God. However, this trust and *faith* would be constantly tested and developed to the very end of his life. God would be developing the kind of *faith* upon which He would build a special people for Himself, and the kind of *faith* that would save all people eternally.

Stop and take time to read Romans 4:1–5:11 to see God's eternal plan to establish faith. After reading, write at least five key thoughts that God showed you through the Scriptures.

____

____

____

____

____

____

____

____

____

____

____

This *faith* is the kind and quality of *faith* developed in Abram by God, to be experienced by all whom He would call His children. Abram's *faith* became the standard for the only kind of *faith* that is acceptable to God for righteousness. We will see how God develops this, as we look carefully at God's activity in the life of Abram—God's "friend."

Abram traveled as far as Haran, in the north, and his father, Terah, chose to dwell there. Maybe Terah knew he was not well. The very next verse said, "And Terah died in Haran" (Gen. 11:32). Sometimes God has to "remove" others from our lives, so He can continue His purposes for our lives.

I was attending seminary when my father died. I was in California when my mother died. I deeply loved my parents. They were very special to me. But God

Abram's *faith* became the standard for the only kind of *faith* that is acceptable to God for righteousness.

may have seen something I could never see in His purposes for my life that could have been affected by them. I did not lose them. I will spend eternity with them, and we will rejoice together in all God chose to do through my life. They had the deepest effect on my life as I began my walk with God. Then they "gave me to God" for His purposes. I remember my father saying, "Henry, the greatest honor God has given to your mother and me is for Him to choose you to be one of His servants. We have given you to Him!"

No sooner had John the Baptist declared, "He must increase, but I must decrease" (John 3:30), than God "took him home" (he was beheaded) so Jesus alone could have the preeminence.

Has God called you and then shortly after removed someone dear to you, or moved you far from loved ones? Have you seen this as an expression of God's love to you for the mighty purposes He has to accomplish through you? Do you need to "revisit" that moment in your life and see that time from God's perspective?

I have been with many who graduated from seminary in obedience to His call and claim in their lives. Then came God's further call to leave all and follow Him. They just could not go far from their parents, so they would not obey Him. They sought a ministry assignment close to where they grew up, so they could be close to home. For many, that "call" never came and they are selling insurance to this day. Will God have to remove someone from your life to have total access to you? He may! But He also may not, because He reads your heart. You may not know until you stand before Him what could have been, if you had only had *faith* to obey Him when He commanded you to follow Him.

Will God have to remove someone from your life to have total access to you?

Have you been willing to do whatever God says as an expression of obedience in your life? Are you willing to say to Christ, "You must increase, but I must decrease"? Explain your answer.

____

____

____

Take time to write out your testimony of your walk of faith with God since you have become a Christian. After you have written it, share with someone how God has worked in your life.

____

____

____

- Review what God has shown you through the lesson today.
- Look back over your lesson and take time to underline or highlight key statements that God used to impact your life.
- Write a statement here that God used most in your life today:

- Turn to the end of the chapter and write your statement again. This will provide a weekly list of key statements for you to meditate on the last two days of the week.

  ❑ CHECK THIS BOX AFTER YOU HAVE DONE SO.
- Take time to pray, asking God to adjust your life to how He has spoken to you today.
- With whom do you need to share this truth today?

SUMMARY STATEMENTS

- Trust and faith will be constantly tested and developed to the very end of life.
- "He must increase, but I must decrease" (John 3:30), so Jesus alone can have the preeminence.
- Obedience, based on faith already established, is crucial!

KEY STATEMENTS FOR MEDITATION

Day 1

Day 2

Day 3

Day 4

Day 5

UNIT 4

A RENEWAL AND ESTABLISHING OF GOD'S "CALL"

THOUGHT STARTER

So Abram departed as the LORD had spoken to him, and Lot went with him. And Abram was seventy-five years old when he departed from Haran.

GENESIS 12:4

HOW VERY SIMPLE AND CLEAR and unmistakable are the ways of God. A child could see them and understand them. The Scriptures merely indicate that God said,

Get out of your country,
From your family
And from your father's house,
To a land that I will show you.

GENESIS 12:1

Abram heard this clearly and God made a Covenant with him. The Covenant is then stated simply and clearly. It then says, "So Abram departed as the LORD had spoken to him." Abram's faith continues and continues to grow. God is pursuing him relentlessly—and lovingly. The "call" first heard in Ur is now being restated afresh. This would be a recurring pattern all through the life of Abram, to the very end. Each restatement would bring with it more revelation, especially about God, and a greater understanding to Abram about the ways of God.

Would you leave your country and family to follow God?

How very simple and clear and unmistakable are the ways of God.

DAY 1

A Covenant with God

Abram's obedience to God in leaving Ur did something special in his relationship with God. God had His Heart set on Abram, and Abram now had his *heart* set on obedience with God. God saw his obedience and his heart, and immediately established a *Covenant* with him. This is one of the most holy and sensitive moments, revealed by God, in all of Scripture. It is so fundamental and basic to anyone's walk with God, especially from God's perspective! God's people are a people not of "vision" but of revelation (that is, what God *reveals* of His will). God now opens His Heart to Abram, to reveal what is on the Heart of God. Though Abram did not fully understand it, it was very simple and very real. But it could be understood only by *experience*—one day at a time and one step of *faith* at a time. Here is a look at the *Covenant* God made with Abram. The elements of this *Covenant* are found all throughout the Scriptures, and are filled full of meaning through the life of Jesus, in the New Testament (New Covenant).

"GET OUT OF YOUR COUNTRY . . . TO A LAND THAT I WILL SHOW YOU"

"You cannot stay in your country and go with Me," was God's word to Abram. God was saying, "Any country, any place won't do! You must go to My country. It is *there* that I will shape you and make you 'My friend.' It is there that I will keep My *Covenant* with you. It will be a land that I will show you." God had "His" country prepared in eternity for His people and His purposes. This is true to this very day. Abram was simply to be the first to "possess" it as a promised gift of God.

This is one of the "ways" of God. It is true with each of His children. Any place will not do with God. Absolute obedience to His directives is essential to God's fulfilling His purposes.

There appears to be no discussion or argument or selfish reasoning on the part of Abram! After the *Covenant* was shared, it simply says, "So Abram departed as the LORD had spoken to him" (Gen. 12:4). The *faith* God is looking for is now being lived out in His servant and "friend" Abram. He was seventy-five years old! To God, Abram had "set his heart" to obey his Lord! Later, King Rehoboam did not "prepare [set] his heart to seek the LORD" and therefore "he did evil" (2 Chron. 12:14), and his life and reign were utter disasters. Without heeding the counsel of God, as Abram did, Rehoboam divided the people of God into two kingdoms. He set in motion the directions for the utter destruction of both kingdoms. Absolute obedience is in fact a matter of life and death, and has eternal consequences.

Absolute obedience is in fact a matter of life and death, and has eternal consequences.

Later on in Jesus' ministry, the disciples had to be *with* Jesus to experience God mightily at work. They had to be where He was to experience God's presence and power, and to be shaped by Him for His use! Jesus said to Peter, "Follow Me, and I will make you become . . ." (Mark 1:17). The first step toward being a "friend of God" is obedience to "follow Him" wherever He commands, wherever He goes, and wherever He should direct. This Abram did faithfully, and God began to unfold what He was going to do in his life.

The first step toward being a "friend of God" is obedience to "follow Him" wherever He commands, wherever He goes, and wherever He should direct.

I certainly faced this kind of moment. Every person called of God to missions faces this also. The call to "get out of your country, from your family, and from your father's house" came hard to me. I was called to be on mission with God the rest of my life. I clearly knew it meant leaving my country—Canada—and going with God to Golden Gate Seminary in California. My father and mother were older than most, and I wanted to spend some of my adult life with them. It was not to be so. I wandered out alone under the stars and cried out to God. His reply: "You are Mine and I am Lord! Now is the time to leave all and follow Me!" After many tears my answer was, "Yes, Lord!" So, like Abram, I left as God had directed me! It was indeed God's timing, and California was indeed God's place. My entire life and ministry would be dramatically shaped over the next thirteen years in California.

Are you willing for God to do anything to shape and mold your life? If you are, explain how you know that. If you are not, explain what is keeping you from that kind of relationship with God.

____

____

____

____

____

____

"I WILL MAKE YOU . . ."

God, in His *Covenant*, promised to become intimately involved in the life of Abram. This was a first! But it would become a sample of what God had purposed to be in the life of anyone who would place his or her faith in Him, as Abram did. God would be like a Potter, and Abram would be the clay. God was saying that He had chosen Abram to be "His friend," and that He would work in him until He had completed this promise. Abram was to trust Him and obey Him. God would do the rest. It would be God who would be at work in Abram, causing him "both to will and to do for His good pleasure" (Phil. 2:13).

Abram would be "His workmanship, created . . . for good works, which God prepared beforehand that [he] should walk in them" (Eph. 2:10).[1] Once this *Covenant* was given and established, the rest of Abram's life can be understood only when you see it from God's perspective and activity. He is working out His purpose in Abram, to make him "His friend." This experience is open to anyone whom God encounters. This is why God said that the one thing He wants from us is to "love the LORD your God with all your heart, with all your soul, and with all your strength" (Deut. 6:5).

Love involves a release of one's life unconditionally to Him, for Him alone.

Love involves a release of one's life unconditionally to Him, for Him alone. When this is in place, God will make you, mold and shape you into exactly what He had in mind for you in eternity, to be lived out in time. When Abram knew this, there was no hesitation, for he knew what God had planned for his life was absolutely best. He would welcome all God had in mind for him.

What was the last thing God asked you to obey in which you obeyed immediately?

___

___

___

For the God of the universe to invite you to let Him shape your life is incredible! Your life could never reach its maximum potential without God! But He loves you and is committed to bring to you His best!

Another picture in the Scriptures of molding a life, especially in the New Testament, is that of a newborn baby. Once the child is born, the parent takes great joy in extending every effort to help and shape that little one's life to reach maximum potential. When we held each of our children for the first time, it was awesome! The birth had happened; now the process of growth had begun. When God is our Father, we are in good hands! He will faithfully bring to us all we need for growth and maturity! But the pilgrimage from birth to maturity takes time and is full of dangers. It also involves learning to work through failures. The world will press us to go its way, and God will love us and draw us to go His way. But His words "I will make you . . ." bring wonderful assurance and anticipation. It is the process that we must learn to handle.

I knew when I held my oldest child that he had the potential to earn a

Ph.D. (his father's expectations) and do great things with God. We set our hearts, even before he could understand, to assure him that we would do everything possible to "help him become . . ." He did earn a Ph.D., and he is doing great things with God, bringing joy to us as parents. If we as weak, sinful parents would help him become, what are the dimensions of a perfect heavenly Father's ability to help each of us become out of His love for us?

- **Review what God has shown you through the lesson today.**
- **Look back over your lesson and take time to underline or highlight key statements that God used to impact your life.**
- **Write a statement here that God used most in your life today:**

____

____

____

- **Turn to the end of the chapter and write your statement again. This will provide a weekly list of key statements for you to meditate on the last two days of the week.**

  ❑ CHECK THIS BOX AFTER YOU HAVE DONE SO.
- **Take time to pray, asking God to adjust your life to how He has spoken to you today.**
- **With whom do you need to share this truth today?**

____

SUMMARY STATEMENTS

- God's ways are simple, clear, and unmistakable.
- Absolute obedience to His directives is essential to God's fulfilling His purposes.
- The first step toward being a "friend of God" is obedience to "follow Him" wherever He commands, wherever He goes, and wherever He should direct.
- Love involves a release of one's life unconditionally to Him, for Him alone.

DAY 2

"I Will Make You a Great Nation"

From creation, Genesis 1, when God speaks, it is so, and it is good! This was true in creation (Gen. 1). This would be true in Abram's life. This is always true with God!

God was now making an incredible promise. He would make through Abram "a great nation"! To be certain, this was something only God could do. But He was God and could do it! Such a Covenant promise from God expressed God's nature—"exceedingly abundantly above all that we ask or think" (Eph. 3:20). If the people of God and the world were to come to know God, He would have to do such great things that all would know it was God and would know the nature of God who was at work in their midst. In love, God would do what was impossible for man to do. The one through whom He would do it would enter into the most intimate relation with God possible to man. For Abram to believe God, and His promise, would endear him to God, and God is always greatly honored when we believe His God-sized promises and obey His directives.

Jesus expressed the connection between God promising to do what is impossible through a person responding by *faith* and *obedience*—and the Father being greatly honored:

> *"Most assuredly, I say to you, he who believes in Me, the works that I do he will do also; and greater works than these he will do, because I go to My Father. And whatever you ask in My name, that I will do, that the Father may be glorified in the Son. If you ask anything in My name, I will do it."*
>
> John 14:12–14

Jesus stated this again, emphatically,

> *"If you abide in Me, and My words abide in you, you will ask what you desire, and it shall be done for you. By this My Father is glorified, that you bear much fruit; so you will be My disciples."*
>
> John 15:7–8

And even more significantly Jesus connected faith and obedience with "being His friend" (as Abram became to God) when He said, "You are My friends if you do whatever I command you" (John 15:14).

But such a promise as this carried with it a great measure of faith by Abram. He had two factors that only God could resolve. He had no child, and he was seventy-five years old. But God had spoken, and Abram knew that it would be so. To Abram, it was impossible for God to speak and not accomplish it, as He promised. How God would accomplish this would shape Abram's faith in God severely. God had to make Abram know that

> *My thoughts are not your thoughts,*
> *Nor are your ways My ways . . .*
> *For as the heavens are higher than the earth,*
> *So are My ways higher than your ways,*
> *And My thoughts than your thoughts.*
>
> ISAIAH 55:8–9

All through his life, this truth would be clearly established, as Abram came to know God more and more completely. But only a trusting *obedience* would bring him to this kind of intimacy with God. The more Abram trusted God and obeyed Him, the more God did to him what He had promised; and the more he knew God, the closer God became to him. *Faith* is based on what you know of God. The more you know Him in experience, the more you can trust Him.

The more Abram trusted God and obeyed Him, the more God did to him what He had promised; and the more he knew God, the closer God became to him.

Since faith is based on what you know of God, how could you improve your knowledge and experience of God?

____

____

____

***Faith* is based on what you know of God.**

Daily *obedience* to God, regardless of what God is asking or promising, is a key to an intimate relationship with God. Since He is God, the only response that is worthy of Him is, "Yes, LORD!" To fail to respond in *obedience* is to fail to experience God's eternal best for our lives. On the other hand, to appropriate every promise God has made (2 Cor. 1:20) is to know by experience the fullness of God (Eph. 3:19–20). Jesus also kept assuring His disciples that if they loved Him, they would obey Him. The response of God to such love from each person would be that both the Father and the Son would "come to him and

Daily *obedience* to God, regardless of what God is asking or promising, is a key to an intimate relationship with God.

make Our home with him," and he would be "loved by My Father, and I will love him and manifest Myself to him" (John 14:23, 21).

This is exactly what Abram would experience in his walk with God. This is what you, too, will experience in your walk with God. God, through Abram, gave us such a simple and clear example of what it means to walk in faith with God. Abram did it in such a way that He would call him "His friend"! It would be appropriate at this point to indicate again that this is precisely what Jesus said to His disciples: "You are My friends if you do whatever I command you." Did you notice the connection between a "friendship" with God in Jesus Christ and *obedience*—doing whatever He commanded us? The similarities between Abram's walk with God and the disciples of Jesus are thorough. Jesus added, "You did not choose Me, but I chose you and appointed you that you should go and bear fruit, and that your fruit should remain" (John 15:14, 16)—just as God did with Abram.

God made a promise to Abram that He would "make him a great nation." Little did Abram know that this nation would be "a special treasure to [God] . . . a kingdom of priests and a holy nation" (Ex. 19:5–6), and that through this nation only would come the Messiah, the Savior. This would be God's loving provision for the sin of the world. Abram couldn't have known this yet. He just had a promise of God. God always does "exceedingly abundantly above all that we ask or think" (Eph. 3:20).

Just a promise from God! But when *faith* appropriates a promise from God, it is done; it is accomplished.

Just a promise from God! But when *faith* appropriates a promise from God, it is done; it is accomplished. The writer of Hebrews defined *faith* exactly this way:

> *Now faith is the assurance (the confirmation, the title deed) of the things [we] hope for, being the proof of things [we] do not see and the conviction of their reality [faith perceiving as real fact what is not revealed to the senses].*
>
> **HEBREWS 11:1 (AMPLIFIED)**

I sat in a pastor's office and heard him describe "the promise of revival" coming to Saskatoon. This promise came from God, through His servant Duncan Campbell, the year before. As I heard the wonderful account, everything within me sensed God giving me a promise: "I will do such a work here. You need to believe Me and appropriate this promise by moving to this city and joining My servants as they pray!"

At that moment I was in the city in view of a call to consider coming to be the pastor of a Baptist church. I did respond to what I was convinced was a word from my Lord for my life. We moved to Saskatoon, and immediately began to pray with several other pastors regularly, including the pastor I had talked to. It was not long (a couple of years) before God poured out His Spirit in significant revival on this pastor's church, and on the entire city. The next seven and one-half weeks were glorious. It has since been constantly referred to as "The Canadian Revival."[2] The experience was beyond all we could ask or think, and the effects of those months are being felt to this day more than twenty-five years later. My life has certainly never been the same!

How important it is that we believe Him, and obey Him immediately and thoroughly, especially when He "makes a promise" to us!

How are you giving careful daily responses to God's working in you?

- **Review what God has shown you through the lesson today.**
- **Look back over your lesson and take time to underline or highlight key statements that God used to impact your life.**
- **Write a statement here that God used most in your life today:**

- **Turn to the end of the chapter and write your statement again. This will provide a weekly list of key statements for you to meditate on the last two days of the week.**

  ❑ CHECK THIS BOX AFTER YOU HAVE DONE SO.
- **Take time to pray, asking God to adjust your life to how He has spoken to you today.**
- **With whom do you need to share this truth today?**

SUMMARY STATEMENTS

- The more Abram trusted God and obeyed Him, the more God did to him what He had promised; and the more he knew God, the closer God became to him.
- Faith is based on what you know of God.
- Daily obedience to God, regardless of what God is asking or promising, is a key to an intimate relationship with God.
- Just a promise from God! But when faith appropriates a promise from God, it is done; it is accomplished.

DAY 3

"I Will Bless You"

What a promise from Almighty God! A personal interest in one of His Own to such an extent that He would promise to "bless" him. And God's capacity to "bless" matches His nature.

God's capacity to "bless" matches His nature.

He is Sovereign, so nothing can prevent Him from doing all He pleases. He is all-powerful, so He can do anything He chooses to do. He is all-knowing, so He has an infinite and measureless capacity to bless. He is all-loving, so there is no limit to what He will do—in love. Each of the Names of God expresses the nature and therefore His capacity to bless. When God announces, "I will bless you!" the mind and heart cannot possibly grasp even its basic meaning. Abram was about to enter a relationship with God in which to be "His friend" would overwhelm him. It would also give His children through all the ages a sample of what God could and would do in their own lives, if they were to believe as Abram did.

In so many ways, Abram's life would become a demonstration of what it means for God to bless a person—in love. God's intimacy with Abram would become encouragement and hope for any that would follow Him in their lives and put their trust in Him. God had promised to pour His life into Abram's, in a similar manner that Jesus promised in John 15, in the picture of the Vine and the branches.

Jesus assured His disciples that if they would "abide" in the Vine (Jesus), they would "bear much fruit" (John 15:7–8). Why? Because He Himself would "abide" in them (live out His life in them). All He was, and all He could do, would become real and personal in their lives. Jesus also told them to let His words "abide" in them (John 15:7). That is, listen to all He says, obey, and His life and love would flow in them and through them. When they did this, God the Father would be clearly known and experienced extensively in them.

His life would literally flow in them and bring much fruit through them. For God to bless Abram would mean that God would also protect Abram when he made mistakes; He would protect him when enemies came against him, or when others purposed to hurt him; He would guide him from place to place, and gently speak to his heart and assure him in ever-increasing measure of His *Covenant* promises. The world would forever know what happens in a person "God calls His friend"!

"I WILL . . . MAKE YOUR NAME GREAT"

Here is a "key" to Abram's life—his *name*! A person's name was his character, the essence of his being. It is what he is in his *heart*! A person's heart determines everything coming out of his life. It is here that God made a promise to develop and shape and mold his *character*, and thereby determine his destiny, especially with God. When the heart is pure, the life is pure, and therefore usable by God for His purposes. What a promise!

Abram's name, his reputation and stature in the eyes of God and men, would literally be "shaped by God's activity"! The blessings of obedience are immeasurable! *Faith* that obeys is God's "key" that unlocks countless blessings! The greatest blessing seems to be what God does *in* us! The heart determines what God can, and will, do through us in our world. So God promises to work *in* us, to develop the kind of *character* that He can bless! It is all the work of God, yet it requires our obedience to what He does in us. He will guide us—and we must obey; He will discipline us, for holiness (Heb. 12:10, 14), so we can see God; He will instruct us, so we can know and do His will—which brings increased blessing; He will reveal Himself to us—so we can love and obey Him, and receive everything His love can provide for us (John 14:12–18, 21, 23); He will command us, so as we obey we will remain in His love (John 15:9–10); and He will share this, so that "joy may remain in [us], and that [our] joy may be full" (John 15:11). Abram experienced this in full—and so may we. God desires to develop our character that we may experience His fullness in us.

The blessings of obedience are immeasurable!

How would you explain to someone how character affects your life?

____

____

____

____

____

____

____

I have often heard my wife say that she believed God moved us to Saskatoon so we could live out, in real life, all we said we believed about God. Everything we said we believed about God would now be tested and made into character in us by the Loving Hand of God. I had always told God's people to trust God to provide all their needs. Now we were where only God could provide for us. God would have to provide everything for our family, for there were only twenty people now in our church. We did trust Him, and He did become "our Provider" for the twelve years that we were pastoring there. He was also our Protector. We came to know this in real life when we traveled to our missions with the wind chill temperature at –110° as the blizzards blew across the roads. He did protect us, and we never were stranded in twelve years of traveling to our missions (more than 500,000 miles). He said He was our Healer, but never did He become so real as Healer than during those early days, especially when my wife almost died, and in the times when He healed our broken hearts. We saw Him shape our very character as He made Himself real and personal. But He always did this in very real-life situations.

God's promise to develop Abram's character was not merely so that Abram could be prosperous in the eyes of his peers. He did become wealthy and prosperous, but so do evil men, men of questionable character. For God to make Abram's name "great" was much more significant than wealth and influence. God would make his name "famous *and* distinguished" (AMPLIFIED). His name would be revered through all of history! God would develop his character to such a degree that God could use Abram as a sample of what He would want all of His children to be like! His name (character) would be the standard for all God's people, especially in his relationship with God. It would be God who would grant him *faith*, and Abram would respond by genuinely trusting God. It would be a process, with some failures, but God promised He would persist in Abram until his character was complete.

The key was not so much how Abram "walked with God" as it was how God walked with Abram.

The key was not so much how Abram "walked with God" as it was how God walked with Abram. Again, it is like the Shepherd and His sheep. The sheep would be the product of the faithfulness of the Shepherd, and not so much how the sheep obeyed the Shepherd. The sheep had to decide to follow the Shepherd, but it was the Shepherd who would make them "lie down in green pastures" in safety, rest, and peace. It was the Shepherd who would lead them "beside the still waters" and provide life-giving water. It was the Shepherd who unafraid would lead them "in the paths of righteousness," and it would be "for His name's sake" (for giving the fullest meaning to His name). The Shepherd would walk them "through the valley of the shadow of death" so they would "fear no evil." The Shepherd would be with them for protection, encouragement, and discipline. It was the Shepherd who would with confidence face their enemy and would bless them. He, the Shepherd, would be with them always and extend to them "goodness and mercy." The character and health of the sheep were the product of the Shepherd's faithfulness. The sheep had to obey and follow, but everything else that affected their character depended on the Shepherd.

For Abram to become "a friend of God," God Himself would have to develop, over time, his character. The rest of the life of Abram is the record of God's activity in his life. His name would stir the greatest motivation for the hearts of the most serious-minded of God's people for the rest of time. *Character determines relationship—and relationship determines character!* It is a paradox, but it is real life!

I have watched God develop character in each of my children. I have watched them as both men and God entrust more and more leadership roles to them. It is the gracious work of a loving, Covenant-keeping God who is faithfully at work in our family. But each of us must recognize God at work and in *faith* obey Him. He does it all—as we respond to Him.

Do you notice what He is doing in your life? Do you realize how much your character (name) affects your life? Are you giving careful daily responses to God's working in you? Your response to His activity is dramatically shaping your life—right now!

- **Review what God has shown you through the lesson today.**
- **Look back over your lesson and take time to underline or highlight key statements that God used to impact your life.**
- **Write a statement here that God used most in your life today:**

____

____

____

- **Turn to the end of the chapter and write your statement again. This will provide a weekly list of key statements for you to meditate on the last two days of the week.**

  ❑ CHECK THIS BOX AFTER YOU HAVE DONE SO.
- **Take time to pray, asking God to adjust your life to how He has spoken to you today.**
- **With whom do you need to share this truth today?**

____

SUMMARY STATEMENTS

- God's capacity to "bless" matches His nature.
- The blessings of obedience are immeasurable!
- The key was not so much how Abram "walked with God" as it was how God walked with Abram.

DAY 4

"You Shall Be a Blessing"

The person God blesses automatically affects those around him and those who are associated with him. As God blessed Abram, so his wife shared in that blessing. As God worked in Abram, so Lot experienced God's blessing in many ways and many places. God expressly affirmed this for Lot and indicated that what He was doing for Lot was because of His blessing of Abram: "When God destroyed the cities of the plain, . . . God remembered Abraham, and sent Lot out of the midst of the overthrow, when He overthrew the cities in which Lot had dwelt" (Gen. 19:29). Many a disaster that could have come in one life was averted because God made a promise with another of His children.

When God said, "You shall be a blessing," God meant that He would bring great blessing on others through him. Because of the intimacy of God's presence in Abram, He would always be present in him and would work through him to effect a blessing on others.

I have been so deeply aware of God's presence and activity in my life. Because of this, and my growing understanding through God's dealings with Abram, I have experienced my life as a "blessing" to others. My wife and I have, at the request of many childless couples, prayed for them to be given a child by God. Later, many have come up to us holding a beautiful child and thanked us "for being such a blessing to them!" This is the covenant promise of God to His children that "you shall be a blessing." Our home is where God has blessed so many people through us.

When I wrote *Experiencing God,* little did I realize how this act of obedience in my life could bring such blessing to so many. While I was speaking on a university campus, a young woman, a student, came up to me and said, "I want to thank you for saving my life." I was rather surprised and inquired further. She said she was going across campus determined to take her life in suicide when another girl compelled her to go to a group that was studying *Experiencing God.* She said this was the turning point in her life. She encountered God there, responded to Him, and He saved her. She said she just had to tell me how my life had saved her. It was obvious I was a "blessing" to her.

Moses became the salvation of many of the children of Israel, because God listened to Moses' prayer of intercession. Many a life was spared because of Samuel, or one of the prophets. And this was supremely true with those who associated with Jesus. His life, totally yielded to God, blessed so many who encountered Him because of the Father in Him. His life let God flow through Him to bless others.

It should also be noted that all the descendants of Abram would be blessed, because of God's blessing Abram. This was true for Ishmael, too: "I will also make a nation of the son of the bondwoman, because he is your seed" (Gen. 21:13). God had made a promise to Abram, and He kept it, that Abram would be a blessing, and he was—over and over again. This is true of any child of God who chooses to walk faithfully and obediently with God. Paul knew this, and assured the Corinthian believers that we are "the aroma of life" to others. Knowing this, he said, "And who is sufficient for these things?" (2 Cor. 2:16).

Paul lived this truth throughout his life. He watched individuals be greatly blessed by their relationship with him in the Gospel. He shared freely how whole churches were experiencing God's blessing because God led Paul to initiate a church where they were.

In addition, Paul's presence brought safety to those on the ship that was wrecked in a storm (Acts 27:23–25). But this truth was not limited to Paul. The very presence of Peter and John brought healing to the disabled man at the temple (Acts 3:1–8).

I remember hearing of a vigilante group being formed in our neighborhood to protect their families and property from what they perceived to be an undesirable element in our community. I received a phone call about this meeting (to which I had not been invited, because we had been out of town). The caller said, "Henry, if you are here, they won't do anything foolish. They are planning to take their guns and stand guard on their property. Please come. Your presence will make a crucial difference!"

Your presence will make a crucial difference!

My wife and I went, and my "presence" under God's leadership made the difference. They did not take up their guns. A peaceful and redemptive solution was made, and the community had peace! Just as God promised Abram that he would be a blessing, so I believed God and He made my life a blessing, too.

We have prayed for wayward children to "return" to the parents, and they have. We have seen finances given, health restored, and revival come—through our presence among God's people.

In addition, we have seen hundreds of marriages saved, and because of this, great joy comes to the entire home and God's Kingdom extended to the ends of the earth. "Saved marriages" have often produced such a presence of the Lord that one or more of the children have felt the call of God into ministry or missions. Many, for whom we have prayed and worked to return to the Lord, have returned and almost immediately sensed God's call into ministry or missions and are now serving Him faithfully.

In so many wonderful ways, from this promise of God, one can trace God's activity making Abram a great blessing to others. We will seek to trace each of the promises made to Abram by God so you may have freedom to expect and recognize God's working in and through your life!

This one promise is significant in our day of great turmoil and uncertainty and fear. Appropriate this promise into your life and family and church, and watch God make you a blessing, too.

Take a moment to reflect on your life. Write a specific situation where God used your presence under God's leadership to bless others.

____

____

____

"I WILL BLESS THOSE WHO BLESS YOU, AND I WILL CURSE HIM WHO CURSES YOU"

This *Covenant* made by God with Abram had far-reaching consequences. No one could touch Abram, without touching God. God had chosen and called him. Even if the person were unaware of who Abram was with God, his life would be in grave and immediate danger if he treated Abram badly. The pharaoh in Egypt put his life and family and nation in jeopardy, because he was about to touch Abram's wife, Sarai (Gen. 12:10–20). All who "blessed" Abram were also blessed by God, such as Abimelech (Gen. 20:1–17; 21:22–33).

Great consequences are also seen in the life of Moses, whom God had chosen. This became painfully clear to Miriam and Aaron when they opposed Moses' leadership. God sent leprosy on Miriam for her rebellion against Moses (Num. 12:1–10). And God restored Miriam to full health through Moses' interceding before God.

There have been many, in my lifetime, who opposed (some vigorously and unfairly) what our church and I knew to be clearly God's will in our lives. I trembled, for I knew that if indeed they were opposing what was of God, He would not leave them untouched.

The first time I experienced such a move of God, I wept and trembled just to realize that when God called me, and I responded, God would affect others by their response to me. This was not because of who I was, but because when God makes a Covenant with His servant, it will look like His Covenant expressed to Abram.

A man in one of the churches I pastored was greatly and persistently disruptive. There came a moment when he could have caused many to leave our church. I cried unto the Lord, and God gave me no freedom to speak with the man. I was surprised! The night before this special moment this man became suddenly and violently ill and was hospitalized. He never again stepped into the church building. He died several weeks later. I fell on my face before God and trembled. But God assured me of the nature of His Covenant—expressed to Abram.

My life would be His Presence among His people. As long as I remained obedient to Him, He would relate personally to all who related to me. I never got over that moment. I took God's call on my life very seriously! I prayed for those who opposed (in an ungodly way) what both others and I knew to be His will. All through my ministry I have been witness to this aspect of God's Covenant with the one He calls to serve Him. To this day I tremble being a chosen servant of God in the midst of His people. I never try to vindicate my integrity with others. God does that, thoroughly.

To this day some of those who opposed God's working in us are not serving God, and much in their lives and families is brokenness and pain and loss. It is frightening to ignore one of the ways of God, especially when He enters into *Covenant* with one He chooses.

My life would be His Presence among His people. As long as I remained obedient to Him, He would relate personally to all who related to me.

It is frightening to ignore one of the ways of God, especially when He enters into *Covenant* with one He chooses.

- **Review what God has shown you through the lesson today.**
- **Look back over your lesson and take time to underline or highlight key statements that God used to impact your life.**
- **Write a statement here that God used most in your life today:**

____

____

____

____

- **Turn to the end of the chapter and write your statement again. This will provide a weekly list of key statements for you to meditate on the last two days of the week.**

  ❑ CHECK THIS BOX AFTER YOU HAVE DONE SO.
- **Take time to pray, asking God to adjust your life to how He has spoken to you today.**
- **With whom do you need to share this truth today?**

____

Summary Statements

- Your presence under God's leadership will make a crucial difference!
- Your life will be God's Presence among His people. As long as you remain obedient to Him, He will relate personally to all who relate to you.
- It is frightening to ignore one of the ways of God, especially when He enters into Covenant with one He chooses.

DAY 5

"And in You All the Families of the Earth Shall Be Blessed"

His purpose in choosing, calling, and shaping Abram's life as a man of *faith* was that through him and his descendants God would bless "all the families of the earth."

Here is the heart of the eternal purpose of God, first expressed to Abram. His purpose in choosing, calling, and shaping Abram's life as a man of *faith* was that through him and his descendants God would bless "all the families of the earth." The great Redemptive and Missionary Heart of God is now revealed to Abram. God deliberately gave him a vision, or revelation, that is of such magnitude that throughout all of his life he would struggle to understand. Even then he would have only a glimpse of what God had in mind, and it would take the rest of history, revealed in the Scriptures, to unfold God's eternal plan to redeem a lost world through him. It would unfold throughout the rest of time. It would be global. It would be all-inclusive. It began with one man through whom God would bring eternal salvation to the whole world. The way He would do it would be seen through Abram's life with God, as God shaped him to be "His friend."

God began with Abram, and announced to him that it would be through him and then through his descendants that He had chosen to bless all the nations of the world. Through Abram and his family, God would build a special people for Himself, a special and holy nation. Through that special people would come the Messiah, the Savior for the whole world and for all in history. Only God could plan such a provision for the sin of the world. Only God could bring it to pass. And only through a man with specific qualities of *faith* would He work to accomplish this. He had found such a man in Abram, and now He had begun His eternal plan, sealing it all in this Special Covenant!

It is important to note the magnitude of the "blessing" He would bring to the nations of the world. Through Abram, He would provide the world with a Savior from sin! God would not merely "bless" them with material things that would pass away. He would bring a Savior who would "save them from their sins" and thus assure them of an eternal life with Him. His eternal purpose was to give each an unlimited, eternal joy in His Presence—forever!

The greatest "blessing" our lives can bring to others and to our world is a Savior who can save them from their sin for all eternity. The Savior, who would be given by God through Abram and his descendants, would be called "JESUS, for He will save His people from their sins" (Matt. 1:21). John later expressed this eternal and global nature of this blessing through Jesus by saying, "He Himself [Jesus] is the propitiation for our sins, and not for ours only but also for the whole world" (1 John 2:2).

The greatest "blessing" our lives can bring to others and to our world is a Savior who can save them from their sin for all eternity.

Tucked in this promised Covenant with Abram was God's eternal plan to save a lost world. Abram was being called to be "on mission with God" in his world. No wonder when God saw Abram's response, He called him "His friend." The eternal salvation of all mankind was at stake!

Have you ever felt the magnitude of God's encounter with you? Have you so sensed *His* eternal purpose through you that you have radically and thoroughly released your will to His will, and your heart to His Heart? Have you been progressively experiencing God's shaping your character to match His assignment in your life? Have you systematically gone through each of the elements in God's *Covenant* with Abram, and compared it as a sample of what He will be doing with your life? Have you talked with your family about your sense of Divine Purpose in your life? Have you shared it with your church? Are you now, trembling, living out a love-relationship with God, through His Son, Jesus Christ, and in the Enabling Power and Presence of His Holy Spirit?

When was the last time you felt the magnitude of God's encounter with you? Share what God did in that encounter.

____

____

____

____

If you are a leader among God's people—a pastor, a staff member, a deacon or elder, a committee chairman, a teacher of His people, or a leader of a larger grouping of His people—have you taught God's people that "the call to salvation" is at the same time a "call to be on mission with God" in our world? Have you taken them through not only the Old Testament Covenants that God made with His people, but also the New Covenant Jesus made with His disciples—in His blood (Matt. 26:28)? Are you as a leader living a life that matches the magnitude of this truth of God?

Will you pause, right now, and respond to God, as you now know Him in His Covenant relationship with you and His people? Write out the basic elements of how you are responding to God.

____

____

____

____

God was ready to take Abram on an extensive journey of *faith* and to develop a man and a nation through which He could bless all the nations of the world. The farther along Abram went with God in this *faith-obedience*, the more God developed his character. As his character changed there came that moment when God changed Abram's *name*—for now he himself was a different person. The new name matched what God had completed in him. His name, Abram ("exalted" or "high one"), was now changed *by God*, who knew Abram's heart, to Abraham—"father of a multitude" or "father of many nations" (Gen. 17:1–8). This was God's goal from the beginning.

The farther along Abram went with God in this *faith-obedience,* the more God developed his character.

Once the character changed, God could fashion the rest of Abraham's life to match His larger assignment. The journey was a long one—twenty-five years before He could trust him with a son, and an additional fifteen years to the place where Abraham faced his greatest and final "test" before God—the sacrifice of his only son from Sarah! God would complete in Abraham what He had begun, for what Abraham became in God's sight would eternally affect all his descendants. The effect of Abraham's *faith* would be spoken of to the end of the Scriptures and the end of time!

Every Christian is chosen, saved, and called by God to be on mission with Him in His world. From the moment a person is saved, God is working to conform him "to the image of His Son" (Rom. 8:28–30). God's purpose, like that for His Son, is to work through us to be a redemptive blessing in others and a redemptive Presence to touch the world. Do you sense clearly that you are "on mission with God" in your world? If you want to know what it would look like in your life to experience God "shaping you to be His friend," study carefully, from God's perspective, the unfolding life of Abraham. Are you ready now to "walk worthy of the calling with which you were called" (Eph. 4:1)?

- Review what God has shown you through the lesson today.
- Look back over your lesson and take time to underline or highlight key statements that God used to impact your life.
- Write a statement here that God used most in your life today:

- Turn to the end of the chapter and write your statement again. This will provide a weekly list of key statements for you to meditate on the last two days of the week.

  ❑ CHECK THIS BOX AFTER YOU HAVE DONE SO.
- Take time to pray, asking God to adjust your life to how He has spoken to you today.
- With whom do you need to share this truth today?

SUMMARY STATEMENTS

- His purpose in choosing, calling, and shaping you as a person of faith is that through you and your descendants God will bless "all the families of the earth."
- The greatest "blessing" our lives can bring to others and to our world is a Savior who can save them from their sin for all eternity.
- The farther along you go with God in faith-obedience, the more God will develop your character.

KEY STATEMENTS FOR MEDITATION

Day 1

Day 2

Day 3

Day 4

Day 5

UNIT 5

ABRAM—SHAPED BY GOD

Thought Starter

ABRAM: LEARNING TO WALK BY FAITH

GOD TAKES THE INITIATIVE to "be involved" in the life of the person God uses, and especially the one He calls "His friend." Sometimes it is by an active intervention. Sometimes it is by mighty acts of His doing. But other times His activity is one of "silence" or nonintervention, or even refusing to stop us when we do not consult Him and we make our own choices without Him. But God is involved in either case! We may tend to sense God is just not involved when He fails to intervene in our wrong decisions. He is indeed vitally involved when He lets us see conclusively that "there is a way that seems right to a man, but its end is the way of death" (Prov. 14:12).

We learn by real-life experiences! We learn also, in real life, when we carefully walk with God's counsel and God's Presence. It seems as though there are stages or steps in God's development of Abram's character and *faith*. This section will see the strategic process God puts Abram through to bring him to another stage in his life. God was building the required foundations, or prerequisites in Abram, before He could trust him further. The key to Abram's development was his clear experience with God Himself. It was the "Nature of God" that Abram must respond to. But God's nature was revealed in real-life experiences! The measure of his *faith* would be directly related to what he knew of God. God would allow famine, family conflict, and outside enemies to severely test him. God would permit extreme moral choices. He would also challenge him to greater *faith* by enlarging His Covenant promises in the face of impossible circumstances. God would also not intervene when Abram listened to human counsel instead of God's promise. Often, Abram's decisions affected permanently, to the end of time, the condition of the entire world. Seen from God's perspective, all this was a vital part of His shaping the man He would use and would ultimately call "His friend." God was far more interested in Abram's *faith* than He was in the consequences of his lack of *faith!*

God was far more interested in Abram's *faith* than He was in the consequences of his lack of *faith!*

DAY 1

Abram Establishes the Covenant in Worship

> *Then the* Lord *appeared to Abram and said, "To your descendants I will give this land." And there he built an altar to the* Lord*, who had appeared to him. And he moved from there to the mountain east of Bethel, and he pitched his tent with Bethel on the west and Ai on the east; there he built an altar to the* Lord *and called on the name of the* Lord*.*
>
> Genesis 12:7–8

God had issued a Covenant with Abram. Now He waited to see how the heart of Abram was set to obey in *faith*! Three responses stand out immediately and are absolutely essential for anyone to walk with God by *faith*. Abram responded immediately, thoroughly, and in *faith*: "So Abram departed as the Lord had spoken to him" (Gen. 12:4). Abram's obedience was immediate, thorough, and full of *faith*!

Abram's obedience was immediate, thorough, and full of *faith!*

Obedience always leads immediately to "walking in the ways of God"! What do you need to do immediately in obedience to God?

____

____

____

____

____

Obedience to the letter was Abram's immediate response. As he heard God he obeyed, and Abram built an altar! God entrusts His Heart and His work to the one who worships Him and does what He commands. God will use an obedient person to bring eternal redemption to His people. Hebrews 11:8 states, "By faith Abraham obeyed when he was called to go out to the place which he would receive as an inheritance. And he went out, not knowing where he was going." This affirms that Abraham had an obedient heart. All through his life God links His activity to Abraham's obedience: "In your seed all the nations of the earth shall be blessed, because you have obeyed My voice" (Gen. 22:18).

And later, God continued the blessing with Isaac, "because Abraham obeyed My voice" (Gen. 26:3–5).

Abram built an altar and worshiped God with all his heart: "And there [Shechem] he built an altar to the LORD, who had appeared to him" (Gen. 12:7). It soon became obvious that worship had been established in his heart.

It was not "blind or ritual" worship. It was "to the LORD, who had appeared to him." His worship was to the God who had called him out of Ur, and out of Haran. And it was to the God who had offered to him a Covenant relationship. There is no record that God had made a covenant with anyone else, so his relationship with God was very special. Abram's worship was very personal and very real, but others began to see an ever-increasing relationship that Abram had with God as he worshiped. His worship was not hidden, but open, so others would make the connection between Abram's worship, the activity and blessing of God, and his growing faith. The Scripture records that Abram "went out, not knowing where he was going" (Heb. 11:8). But the key to such *faith* lies in what the Scripture records next: "And there [Shechem] he built an altar" (Gen. 12:7).

When he moved to Bethel (v. 8), it again records, "There he built an altar to the LORD and called on the name of the LORD." This "pattern of worship" continued throughout his life—except when there was a famine, and he chose to go down to Egypt. Because Abram knew God in his heart, worship was a way of life to him. He constantly anticipated fresh encounters with God throughout his life. And it was in these special moments that God revealed more and more of Himself and His Covenant promise. It was also where Abram was encouraged and invited to make further strides in his walk of *faith*. There is no record of others, even in his family, "building an altar," but it was a mark of Abram's walk with God. Where God spoke, there he built an altar. The altar at Bethel became very special to him, for after he had sinned grievously in Egypt, he knew where he could "return to God"—to the place where God had previously spoken to him, and where he had built an altar. It was Abram's "meeting place with God."

Because Abram knew God in his heart, worship was a way of life to him.

Take time to read all of Genesis 12. It will be helpful for the rest of this week's studies. After reading the chapter, list the elements that God brought full meaning to as you read.

____

____

____

____

____

- **Review what God has shown you through the lesson today.**
- **Look back over your lesson and take time to underline or highlight key statements that God used to impact your life.**
- **Write a statement here that God used most in your life today:**

- **Turn to the end of the chapter and write your statement again. This will provide a weekly list of key statements for you to meditate on the last two days of the week.**

  ❑ CHECK THIS BOX AFTER YOU HAVE DONE SO.
- **Take time to pray, asking God to adjust your life to how He has spoken to you today.**
- **With whom do you need to share this truth today?**

SUMMARY STATEMENTS

- God was far more interested in Abram's faith than He was in the consequences of his lack of faith!
- Abram's obedience was immediate, thorough, and full of faith!
- Because Abram knew God in his heart, worship was a way of life to him.

DAY 2

A HEART FOR WORSHIP

It is preeminently true that no one can be shaped by God and consistently blessed by God who has not established his heart in worship! It is in worship that God has purposed to reveal Himself, in ever-increasing measure. Continually notice how God shapes the mind and heart of Abram as he worships. Worship is a deliberate, steady, focused time with God. Worship anticipates not only an encounter with God, but also a clear next word from God. Worship is totally God-centered! God-focused! Out of worship comes a clearer and more focused relationship of *faith* and *obedience* with God. Worship is God's way of developing character and directing the life into the center of His will. Abram was supremely a worshiper, and his life is a testimony to this fact. The ultimate outcome of consistent worship is a life totally yielded to God, on God's terms.

Worship is a deliberate, steady, focused time with God.

But it is not automatic. It is developed over time, in the midst of all kinds of circumstances and external pressures. That is precisely why worship is so essential. God, who has all knowledge about the present and about the future, desires to shape a person specifically while His chosen servants worship.

The ultimate outcome of consistent worship is a life totally yielded to God, on God's terms.

Worship is a deliberate, steady, focused time with God, when one anticipates not only an encounter with God, but also a clear next word from God for life. What word from God have you received recently in your time of worship?

____

____

____

____

It was while Isaiah was in worship that he encountered God. It was there God made needed corrections in Isaiah's life. Then God revealed His own Heart and purposes to which Isaiah responded immediately, thoroughly, and in complete *faith* when he said,

> *Woe is me, for I am undone!*
> *Because I am a man of unclean lips,*
> *And I dwell in the midst of a people of unclean lips;*
> *For my eyes have seen the King,*
> *The* LORD *of hosts.*
>
> ISAIAH 6:5

The process continued with Isaiah, and once cleansed by God, he would hear God:

Also I heard the voice of the Lord, saying:
"Whom shall I send,
And who will go for Us?"

ISAIAH 6:8

Isaiah had been so changed by his worship encounter with God that when he heard God speak, his answer was immediate, thorough, and full of *faith*, responding with, "Here am I! Send me" (Isa. 6:8).

Hannah, too, was worshiping in the temple when God encountered her and told of His purpose to grant her a child. He told her the child would be a great deliverer of God's people (1 Sam. 1:8–20).

Turn to 1 Samuel 1 in your Bible. Read the entire chapter. Highlight or underline words, phrases, or verses that reveal how God encountered Hannah. Then write a few sentences that explain what impacted you most when you read about Hannah.

It is so clear in the Scripture how God answered her prayer when you read verse 20: "So it came to pass in the process of time that Hannah conceived and bore a son, and called his name Samuel, saying, 'Because I have asked for him from the LORD.'"

A further most remarkable encounter with God while worshiping came to Zacharias (Luke 1:5–17). It was there that God revealed that he and his wife, Elizabeth, would have a son who would go before the Messiah and prepare the way for Him. The child's name would be John (John the Baptist), "and he will turn many of the children of Israel to the Lord their God" (Luke 1:16).

Again, go to the Scriptures. Read Luke 1:5–17. Highlight or underline words, phrases, or verses that reveal how God encountered Zacharias and Elizabeth. Then write a few sentences that explain what impacted you most when you read about Zacharias and Elizabeth.

Worship always has enormous opportunities for God, in His Own time, to reveal Himself and His immediate purposes to those He has chosen to be His special servants.

It was while I was worshiping that God placed His Hand upon my life for His purposes. And now, after more than forty-seven years, worship has been my special time of meeting with God, when He continues to reveal His will in my life.

Worship always has enormous opportunities for God, in His Own time, to reveal Himself and His immediate purposes to those He has chosen to be His special servants.

- **Review what God has shown you through the lesson today.**
- **Look back over your lesson and take time to underline or highlight key statements that God used to impact your life.**
- **Write a statement here that God used most in your life today:**

- **Turn to the end of the chapter and write your statement again. This will provide a weekly list of key statements for you to meditate on the last two days of the week.**

  ❑ CHECK THIS BOX AFTER YOU HAVE DONE SO.
- **Take time to pray, asking God to adjust your life to how He has spoken to you today.**
- **With whom do you need to share this truth today?**

SUMMARY STATEMENTS

- Worship is a deliberate, steady, focused time with God.
- The ultimate outcome of consistent worship is a life totally yielded to God, on God's terms.
- Worship always has enormous opportunities for God, in His Own time, to reveal Himself and His immediate purposes to those He has chosen to be His special servants.

DAY 3

A Hard Lesson in Egypt (part 1)

God shapes the ones He chooses by often allowing dire or serious circumstances to enter life's pilgrimage.

God shapes the ones He chooses by often allowing dire or serious circumstances to enter life's pilgrimage. They are not serious to God. Nothing is serious to God, for in His Sovereignty He is always in complete control. But to the ones who are learning to walk with Him, circumstances often test us severely. Yet God, who has made a Covenant, is present to fulfill His promise. He will ultimately intervene and will save and will in the process teach us (1) His nature; (2) our total need of Him; (3) His *ways* in our lives; and (4) His personal care for those our lives are affecting. All of these were present in Abram, as we see unfolding in his life the way God shapes the man He calls "His friend."

"Now there was a famine in the land, and Abram went down to Egypt to dwell there, for the famine was severe in the land" (Gen. 12:10). It was a crucial test for Abram's character, especially his *faith* in God. Obedience always leads immediately to the "walking in the *ways* of God"! Paul expressed this truth wonderfully: "Be anxious for nothing, but in everything by prayer and supplication, with thanksgiving, let your requests be made known to God; and the peace of God, which surpasses all understanding, will guard your hearts and minds through Christ Jesus" (Phil. 4:6–7).

Abram had to learn this—and he did so the hard way with potentially costly results. He failed to consult with God in his time of crisis. The famine was real and severe. Human reasoning *without God* would have done what Abram did. But God wanted him to know Him, and His provision and protection, even in famine. God had just promised to "bless" Abram. This means in *all circumstances*, at all times, under all conditions. Abram failed his first "test"—but not utterly.[1] "Going down to Egypt" was not God's way. When the famine worsened, there is no record of Abram "calling on the Name of his God" or trusting Him for guidance. There was no worship recorded, and therefore no "word from God"! Does God permit famine to come to His chosen servants? All the time! But He can never reveal Himself and His provisions and care for His own if we turn to "the world" for its help. How God would have provided, we do not know (in disobedience we never know what *could have been*).

In disobedience we never know what *could have been.*

What was happening in your life when God permitted famine to come to you?

____

____

Have you responded to a sudden change of circumstances that created great concern in your life by taking the counsel of the world or turning to the world for help?

When Abram got to the place of *his* choosing (Egypt),[2] it was not what he had anticipated (it never is). He suddenly became afraid for his life, because of the beauty of his wife. Plotting together, Abram convinced her to take his counsel and say she was his sister, which he felt would protect both of them. God knew that "there is a way that seems right to a man, but its end is the way of death" (Prov. 14:12). It is an absolute with God. Even Jesus expressed this by saying, "Without Me you can do nothing" (John 15:5). Abram had to learn this, and so must we.

There are no shortcuts to obedience of *faith* with God! Either you turn to Him for counsel and obey what He says, or you make your choice in what seems right to you! The latter can be fatal—and almost was for Abram. It is crucial to note that our best thinking—without God—can be fatal to our families and those dear to us who are walking with us! Many people have used their best thinking about their marriages, but never thoroughly sought God's counsel, waited patiently for Him to speak, and obeyed Him. They hurried off to do their own "best thinking" only to discover there was so much they did not know, and so much was truly out of their control. It all too often takes their marriages into fatal divorce, bringing great pain to their families and their friends around them.

It is crucial to note that our best thinking—without God—can be fatal to our families and those dear to us who are walking with us!

- **Review what God has shown you through the lesson today.**
- **Look back over your lesson and take time to underline or highlight key statements that God used to impact your life.**
- **Write a statement here that God used most in your life today:**

- **Turn to the end of the chapter and write your statement again. This will provide a weekly list of key statements for you to meditate on for the last two days of the week.**

  ❑ CHECK THIS BOX AFTER YOU HAVE DONE SO.
- **Take time to pray, asking God to adjust your life to how He has spoken to you today.**
- **With whom do you need to share this truth today?**

SUMMARY STATEMENTS

- God shapes the ones He chooses by often allowing dire or serious circumstances to enter life's pilgrimage.
- In disobedience we never know what could have been.
- It is crucial to note that our best thinking—without God—can be fatal to our families and those dear to us who are walking with us.

DAY 4

A HARD LESSON IN EGYPT (PART 2)

Seeing Abram's life as God saw it, we notice that God was not about to let His servant be destroyed (which genuinely could have happened). God, in His Sovereignty, and in His love and mercy, controls kings and pharaohs, too. Solomon described God's Sovereignty in the lives of kings by saying,

The king's heart is in the hand of the LORD,
Like the rivers of water;
He turns it wherever He wishes.

PROVERBS 21:1

***How* God does it matches the one He is dealing with.**

God has always worked this way, but Abram was about to experience Him doing it! *How* God does it matches the one He is dealing with.

The Scriptures indicate, "The LORD plagued Pharaoh and his house with great plagues because of Sarai, Abram's wife" (Gen. 12:17). This was not merely to alert Pharaoh, but to alert Abram to the awesome influence of his life on others—for good and for evil. Abram's obedience would bring great blessing to others, especially his family; but Abram's disobedience would also bring great harm to others, especially his own family. Pharaoh cried out to Abram, "What is this you have done to me? Why did you not tell me that she was your wife?" (Gen. 12:18). Pharaoh had come terrifyingly face-to-Face with God—and so did Abram and his family. God protects His own, and teaches them about Himself, so they will forever walk with Him in *faith*—*faith* that is full of knowledge. God was shaping the heart and life of Abram, teaching him the significant dimensions of *faith*.

Faith is based on facts—but facts God has granted. When you do not have facts from God, your next step is one not of *faith* but of presumption! God, in mercy and love, intervened, but not directly with Abram, this time. God dealt directly with Pharaoh and sent great plagues to his entire house. God revealed Abram's relationship with God to Pharaoh, and Pharaoh obeyed God and spared Abram. Too often the world is wiser than God's people are—but God will make the corrective in His people.

When you do not have facts from God, your next step is one not of *faith* but of presumption!

Abram was spared, and immediately returned to Bethel, "to the place of the altar which he had made there at first. And there Abram called on the name of the LORD" (Gen. 13:4). Oh, what a meeting that must have been!

There is no record that God asked Abram to confess his sin! As later, Jesus never asked Peter to confess his sin. Jesus asked Peter to confess his love for Him, for if he loved his Lord, all else would be all right. So God waited to see what Abram would do next. To return and worship Him, and call on His Name, would indicate Abram's heart was still trusting God. When a child of God sins, what he does next will reveal his heart-relationship with God! *Faith* in God always returns a person to God for forgiveness. *Faith* always trusts and obeys. The Covenant was still in place. God had not changed. Abram had to know this—by experience!

It is significant that Abram called on the *Name* of the Lord. But by now he knew much more of the Nature of God than before, and his worship now included God as Protector. Now he knew *from personal experience* more of the Covenant that God had made with him. And now, his faith was stronger, and with greater understanding. He would now continue his journey with God, but with a richer and fuller response to God, and a much greater sensitivity to God.

Stop right now, and examine, with careful meditation, your own personal pilgrimage with God. Have you responded to a sudden change of circumstances that created great concern in your life by taking the counsel of the world or turning to the world for help? Did you fail to immediately and instinctively turn to God, and wait on Him for His direction? Are you, right now, in the midst of the consequences of your decision, without the counsel of God? Go back to *your* altar, where you first established a covenant with God, or the last vow you made to God, and restore the relationship with Him through confession of sin, repentance, and appropriation of His forgiveness. Let Him do in you what David asked:

Restore . . . the joy of [My] salvation.

PSALM 51:12

- **Review what God has shown you through the lesson today.**
- **Look back over your lesson and take time to underline or highlight key statements that God used to impact your life.**
- **Write a statement here that God used most in your life today:**

- **Turn to the end of the chapter and write your statement again. This will provide a weekly list of key statements for you to meditate on the last two days of the week.**

  ❑ CHECK THIS BOX AFTER YOU HAVE DONE SO.
- **Take time to pray, asking God to adjust your life to how He has spoken to you today.**
- **With whom do you need to share this truth today?**

SUMMARY STATEMENTS

- How God works matches the one He is dealing with.
- When you do not have facts from God, your next step is one not of faith but of presumption!

DAY 5

CRUCIAL CHOICES BRING EXPANDED BLESSINGS

Unguarded strength is our greatest danger.

Abram had spent time alone with God in worship at his altar in Bethel (Gen. 13:4). It was a high moment for Abram. Forgiven and restored, he faced a bright future! But it should be noted that we always fall from our high points.

Unguarded strength is our greatest danger. Many people go up and down in their Christian life. You cannot fall from the valley; you are already at the bottom. It is at the high points that you have the greatest potential of falling. Our tendency is to relax when we are having the mountaintop experience. Be sure to guard your heart when you are on the mountaintop.

Unguarded strength is our greatest danger. Who are your godly counselors that help you with decisions?

____

____

____

For *faith* to grow and be strengthened, it must pass through moments of choices. And choices always carry with them the matter of "obedience" to God. Abram had no sooner gone through a choice in which he failed than he was faced with another choice, but this time it concerned family. We often like to have a space of time between testing, but we do not determine that; God does. Conflict arose between Abram's herdsmen and Lot's. The heart and character of Abram are *revealed*. Conflict does not *make* character; it *reveals* what's in the heart.

Conflict does not *make* character; it *reveals* what's in the heart.

So Abram said to Lot, "Please let there be no strife between you and me, and between my herdsmen and your herdsmen; for we are brethren. Is not the whole land before you? Please separate from me. If you take the left, then I will go to the right; or, if you go to the right, then I will go to the left" (Gen. 13:8–9).

Conflict does not *make* character; it *reveals* what's in the heart. Is there a conflict happening in your life for which you need clear direction from God in how to respond? If so, write your response.

____

____

____

The bigness of Abram's character came out. He was learning to guard his heart. He was also learning the Heart of God. Worship does that! But once again it is important to notice the activity of God in the midst of choices made. Once Abram was a chosen servant of God, his choices reflected his understanding of that relationship. They had to be made from character, in harmony with the God he served. He passed this test, and God immediately returned to His Covenant and gave Abram more details. For the first time, God showed him the place that God would give to him and to his descendants:

And the Lord *said to Abram, after Lot had separated from him: "Lift your eyes now and look from the place where you are—northward, southward, eastward, and westward; for all the land which you see I give to you and your descendants forever. And I will make your descendants as the dust of the earth; so that if a man could number the dust of the earth, then your descendants also could be numbered. Arise, walk in the land through its length and its width, for I give it to you." Then Abram moved his tent, and went and dwelt by the terebinth trees of Mamre, which are in Hebron, and built an altar there to the* Lord.

Genesis 13:14–18

For the first time Abram knew "the land that I will show you"! He was told he was standing on it. He had waited for God, and God made known His will. Here also reveals an enormous contrast between Abram, who waited on God's choice of land, and Lot, who chose for himself with little or no reference to God. Lot's choice, made in the flesh and human reasoning, placed him near the most wicked cities of his day, Sodom and Gomorrah (Gen. 13:12). History would reveal the consequences of such a choice. The character of Lot would be weakened, but the character of Abram strengthened. Choices will do that. We are free to make the choice, but not free from the consequences of the choice.

We are free to make the choice, but not free from the consequences of the choice.

You are free to make the choice, but not free from the consequences. If you make a wrong choice, what should you do next?

___

___

___

Always take time with God following significant decisions, especially when your decision is based on true *faith,* and your future from that decision requires God to implement it.

For the first time God also added that He would make Abram's descendants as numerous as "the dust of the earth." God was very specific and very timely in this response to Abram's *faith.* He continued to shape the man He would call "His friend."

It is obvious Abram responded deeply to this fresh encounter with God. He moved his tent toward Hebron "and built an altar there to the Lord"! The altars were becoming "spiritual markers" for Abram and his family. They were places where God revealed Himself afresh to His servant and "friend," Abram. And Abram's decision to worship was affecting his family around him.

Always take time with God following significant decisions, especially when your decision is based on true *faith*, and your future from that decision requires

God to implement it. Notice also that again when God spoke to him, he moved to Hebron "and built an altar there" (Gen. 13:18). Worship is always appropriate following a fresh encounter with God. This is always pleasing to God when we acknowledge His activity in our lives.

Each time God has led us to move our family to a new place of service, we, too, have bought a home, dedicated our new dwelling place, and immediately united with a church where we could worship God with all our hearts. Is this your established habit in your walk with God? Your place of worship, immediately upon knowing God's will and new place of service, needs an altar where you and your family can meet God daily!

- **Review what God has shown you through the lesson today.**
- **Look back over your lesson and take time to underline or highlight key statements that God used to impact your life.**
- **Write a statement here that God used most in your life today:**

____

____

____

- **Turn to the end of the chapter and write your statement again. This will provide a weekly list of key statements for you to meditate on the last two days of the week.**

  ❑ CHECK THIS BOX AFTER YOU HAVE DONE SO.
- **Take time to pray, asking God to adjust your life to how He has spoken to you today.**
- **With whom do you need to share this truth today?**

____

SUMMARY STATEMENTS

- Unguarded strength is our greatest danger.
- Conflict does not make character; it reveals what's in the heart.
- We are free to make the choice, but not free from the consequences of the choice.
- Always take time with God following significant decisions, especially when your decision is based on true faith, and your future from that decision requires God to implement it.

KEY STATEMENTS FOR MEDITATION

Day 1

Day 2

Day 3

Day 4

Day 5

UNIT 6

THE COST OF A NEW NAME

Thought Starter

Because you have kept My command to persevere, I also will keep you from the hour of trial which shall come upon the whole world, to test those who dwell on the earth. Behold, I am coming quickly! Hold fast what you have, that no one may take your crown. He who overcomes, I will make him a pillar in the temple of My God, and he shall go out no more. I will write on him the name of My God and the name of the city of My God, the New Jerusalem, which comes down out of heaven from My God. And I will write on him My new name. He who has an ear, let him hear what the Spirit says to the churches.

REVELATION 3:10–13

WHEN A CHILD IS BORN, sensitive parents seek diligently to give their precious child a name, which he will live with all his life. Some names that are given have much "sacred" history to them, and the child may seek to honor the name.

In God's Covenant with us He gives us a name that is special to Him and to us. How then should we live?

DAY 1

Real Battles

I do not pray that You should take them out of the world, but that You should keep them from the evil one. They are not of the world, just as I am not of the world. Sanctify them by Your truth. Your word is truth. As You sent Me into the world, I also have sent them into the world. And for their sakes I sanctify Myself, that they also may be sanctified by the truth.

John 17:15–19

With God, there are no shortcuts to maturity. There is no possibility of avoiding real-life situations.

With God, there are no shortcuts to maturity. There is no possibility of avoiding real-life situations. And life always brings some measure of conflict, even real battles. But God is always with those He chooses to (1) bring them through the battles, (2) bring them to new understanding of Himself, and (3) shape their character in new and fresh ways. Conflicts are God's means of developing character, especially faith in Him.

Jesus prayed to God for His disciples not that God would "take them out of the world," but that God would "keep them from the evil one" (John 17:15). God did not keep Abram *from* battles perpetrated by evil kings, but kept him *in the midst of* battles and conflict, revealing the special blessing that accompanies any person chosen and called by God for His purposes in the world. Real battles, by real enemies, create wonderful opportunities for God to develop character and trust. There are many lessons to learn in life's "battles." But more than anything else, character is tested.

This time of conflict from the world around him did a number of things to refine and develop what God was ultimately looking for in the one whom God had chosen to be "the father of us all [the faithful]" (Rom. 4:16). First the setting: Four powerful kings came against five kings, including the king of Sodom, where Lot lived. Lot *chose* to live close to Sodom, a city "exceedingly wicked and sinful against the LORD" (Gen. 13:13). If you choose to live where God has not directed, and where sin reigns, you have to accept the consequences. All the people and possessions of Sodom, including Lot, were defeated and taken captive.

If you choose to live where God has not directed, and where sin reigns, you have to accept the consequences.

Real battles, by real enemies, create wonderful opportunities for God to develop character and trust. What battle have you gone through?

What character was developed in your life as a result of going through the battle?

In such a time as this, the *Covenant* God made with Abram to "make him a blessing" was exceedingly timely. Abram, though gentle and a peacemaker, was suddenly brought forth as a strong and powerful military leader as well. He took 318 trained servants, three allies and their men, pursued and defeated the victorious kings, and returned Lot and all the captured people and possessions of Sodom. This victory was the first in Abram's new relationship with God. It was very similar to that of Gideon when he defeated the Midianites and the Amalekites who were "lying in the valley as numerous as locusts; and their camels were without number, as the sand by the seashore in multitude" (Judg. 7:12), with only three hundred choice men—plus God!

Conflict reveals character. God knew this but Abram had to learn this. Conflict brought out greatness in Abram as a military strategist. But Abram knew that regardless of his ability, only God could give him the victory. God was watching to see if Abram would take the Glory that belonged to God alone, or would guard God's Glory and not touch it for himself. Would Abram pass the test in all the dangers that lurk in victory?

Conflict reveals character.

- **Review what God has shown you through the lesson today.**
- **Look back over your lesson and take time to underline or highlight key statements that God used to impact your life.**
- **Write a statement here that God used most in your life today:**

- **Turn to the end of the chapter and write your statement again. This will provide a weekly list of key statements for you to meditate on the last two days of the week.**

❑ CHECK THIS BOX AFTER YOU HAVE DONE SO.

- **Take time to pray, asking God to adjust your life to how He has spoken to you today.**
- **With whom do you need to share this truth today?**

Summary Statements

- With God, there are no shortcuts to maturity. There is no possibility of avoiding real-life situations.
- If you choose to live where God has not directed, and where sin reigns, you have to accept the consequences.
- Conflict reveals character.

DAY 2

Real Tests

A greater test came as God trained the heart and character of Abram. A far greater battle faced him in the contrast of two kings who came up to greet him on his victorious return. First, Melchizedek, king of Salem, came and gave Abram a blessing from God Most High, and assured him that it was God who had "delivered [his] enemies into [his] hand" (Gen. 14:18–20).

How wonderful are the ways and the love of God. When God sets His love on one He chooses, He moves carefully and strategically to protect His servant. God sent a messenger to assure Abram—and remind him—that God Himself had brought this unusual victory, for He had promised to bless him.

When God sets His love on one He chooses, He moves carefully and strategically to protect His servant.

Think back to a time when there was a great victory in your life. Make a list of God's messengers who came alongside you to remind you not to take God's Glory for yourself. If no one did come alongside you, give the reason why you believe no one came.

This quality is absolutely essential to being wholly God's! I have faced this forcefully. *Experiencing God,* which He let me write with Claude King, is approaching three million copies sold of the workbook alone. But many, in timely and loving ways, have reminded me that only God could do this! This, I know, is absolutely true. The moment I "take credit," I touch the Glory that belongs to God alone. I risk everything, especially my usefulness to God, if I violate this. "Success" is a grave danger to the heart of every servant of God! "Success" is a severe moment of testing before God. Be careful how you handle it.

Second, the king of Sodom offered Abram all the wealth captured, as a reward. This is the way the "world" responds, but Abram refused any of it, saying, "Lest you should say, 'I have made Abram rich'" (Gen. 14:23). Abram refused to touch the Glory that belonged to God alone—and God was exceedingly pleased with the growing *faith* of His servant. When the heart remains true to God, with trust and confidence in Him alone, God proceeds to reveal more of Himself, thus developing a greater capacity for *faith* in Abram.

"Success" is a grave danger to the heart of every servant of God! "Success" is a severe moment of testing before God. Be careful how you handle it.

When the heart remains true to God, with trust and confidence in Him alone, God proceeds to reveal more of Himself, thus developing a greater capacity for *faith*. Has your heart remained true to God? How would someone know that it has? If your heart has not remained true to God, what adjustments will you make?

____

____

____

____

____

- **Review what God has shown you through the lesson today.**
- **Look back over your lesson and take time to underline or highlight key statements that God used to impact your life.**
- **Write a statement here that God used most in your life today:**

____

____

____

- **Turn to the end of the chapter and write your statement again. This will provide a weekly list of key statements for you to meditate on the last two days of the week.**

  ❑ CHECK THIS BOX AFTER YOU HAVE DONE SO.
- **Take time to pray, asking God to adjust your life to how He has spoken to you today.**

- **With whom do you need to share this truth today?**

Summary Statements

- When God sets His love on one He chooses, He moves carefully and strategically to protect His servant.
- "Success" is a grave danger to the heart of every servant of God!
- "Success" is a severe moment of testing before God. Be careful how you handle it.

DAY 3

God Revealed

God immediately revealed Himself, His Name, in two significant aspects.

First,

Do not be afraid, Abram. I am your shield.

Genesis 15:1

It was indeed God who had protected him and given him the victory. And Abram was now promised perpetual protection by his God, because he had believed God and trusted Him to deliver him.

Second,

Do not be afraid, Abram. I am . . . your exceedingly great reward.

Genesis 15:1

God withholds nothing from those who trust Him.

God Himself would be Abram's heritage. All that was God, including all He could do and all He "possessed," was promised to Abram. God withholds nothing from those who trust Him. The entire rest of the Bible is a witness to the extent and extravagance of God's gifts to those who trust Him. God had said He would make Abram's name great. The name of Abram, and all his wealth, which would be known to all, came from God, not man. Abram wanted this Glory to go to God. He was "God's friend"! And God said that He Himself would be Abram's reward. It would be "exceedingly great" because God had promised it.

It was significant that Abram knew how men would boast, and he would not give the king of Sodom the opportunity to take any credit for God's working through his life.

Faith includes giving God the Glory when He provides "according to His riches in glory by Christ Jesus" (Phil. 4:19), and the "exceeding riches of His grace" (Eph. 2:7). This was a severe test to Abram. He was coming to know, like the Apostle Paul, "of Him and through Him and to Him are all things, to whom be glory forever" (Rom. 11:36). This was the kind of heart and kind of person God was developing as a model for all those who would afterward put their trust in Him. I do not know if Abram knew that this was a test of his *faith*, but God did! And what God did next establishes a pattern for *faith* for all time.

***Faith* includes giving God the Glory when He provides "according to His riches in glory by Christ Jesus" (Phil. 4:19), and the "exceeding riches of His grace" (Eph. 2:7).**

How do you give God the Glory when He provides for you? Think this through thoroughly. **Do you simply give a Christian one-liner like, "I give all Glory to God," or do other people recognize that you give Glory to God by not only what you say but also how you live? How do they recognize your sincere humility?**

____

____

____

____

____

____

The greatest men and women of history have had to develop this character quality! The Apostle Paul said, "To me, who am less than the least of all the saints, this grace was given, that I should preach among the Gentiles the unsearchable riches of Christ" (Eph. 3:8).

Paul knew fully in his day that God did all that was accomplished in others through him. Similarly, many a popular servant of God fell and lost his ministry because of exhibiting pride and taking credit for what God had done. Jesus said, "Without Me you can do nothing" (John 15:5). Since this is true in all of His disciples, at all times, and under all circumstances, it is vitally important to always acknowledge this and do it immediately in the victories He grants to us.

Many a popular servant of God fell and lost his ministry because of exhibiting pride and taking credit for what God had done.

- **Review what God has shown you through the lesson today.**
- **Look back over your lesson and take time to underline or highlight key statements that God used to impact your life.**

- **Write a statement here that God used most in your life today:**

- **Turn to the end of the chapter and write your statement again. This will provide a weekly list of key statements for you to meditate on the last two days of the week.**

  ❑ CHECK THIS BOX AFTER YOU HAVE DONE SO.
- **Take time to pray, asking God to adjust your life to how He has spoken to you today.**
- **With whom do you need to share this truth today?**

SUMMARY STATEMENTS

- God withholds nothing from those who trust Him.
- Faith includes giving God the Glory when He provides "according to His riches in glory by Christ Jesus" (Phil. 4:19), and the "exceeding riches of His grace" (Eph. 2:7).
- Many a popular servant of God fell and lost his ministry because of exhibiting pride and taking credit for what God had done.

DAY 4

ABRAM'S SPIRITUAL CONVERSION

In God's process of developing Abram as His "friend" (James 2:23), no moment in his life was more significant as a "spiritual watershed," or dividing point, than what God did next! God revealed Himself to Abram as being his "shield" and his "exceedingly great reward" (Gen. 15:1).

With every new revelation of God to Abram, Abram's heart grew stronger and bolder with a deeper longing for God. The more God revealed of Himself, the more certain Abram became that he could return to the original promises of God concerning a child. Abram's *faith* was moving strongly to the promise, because he was experiencing more of God Himself.

A lesser person might have been satisfied with this. But Abram immediately pleaded for the "original promise," which required a son, and he remained childless! Abram's *faith* comes out clearly:

Look, You have given me no offspring.

GENESIS 15:3

True *faith* persists until the promise is fulfilled. That is what makes it *faith* that pleases God! God knew He would give Abram a son. He was waiting for Abram's heart to develop where he would persist before God until the son was given. Delayed promises can diminish faith or strengthen faith! Abram was expressing not unbelief, but belief! He just wanted God to assure him of this Covenant promise.

True *faith* persists until the promise is fulfilled. That is what makes it *faith* that pleases God!

Delayed promises can diminish faith or strengthen faith! How do you respond to delayed promises?

____

____

____

Delayed promises can diminish faith or strengthen faith!

Seeing again the *heart* of His servant, Abram, God once more affirmed to him that, indeed,

"one who will come from your own body shall be your heir."

GENESIS 15:4

Then God asked him to look into the night sky and count the stars, if he was able to number them, and assured him, "So shall your descendants be" (Gen. 15:5). Then came the momentous, history-changing words,

And he believed in the LORD, and He accounted it to him for righteousness.

GENESIS 15:6

It was in this declaration that Abram was justified by faith!—a phrase at the heart of Paul's gospel in Romans 4 and Galatians 3. This, and the accompanying and expanding *Covenant,* rather than the covenant on Sinai, was to be the fundamental Covenant God would make with all who would believe. This Covenant expressed grace, and not Law. And it must be mentioned that it was in honoring *this* Covenant that God brought His people out of Egypt: "So God heard their groaning, and God remembered His covenant with Abraham . . . And God looked upon the children of Israel, and God acknowledged them" (Ex. 2:24–25).

It was true also when God brought His Son into the world. Speaking through Zacharias in a fulfilled prophecy, God declared, "He has visited and redeemed His people . . . as He spoke . . . to remember His holy covenant, the oath which He swore to our father Abraham" (Luke 1:68–74). This moment set the pattern of faith for the rest of Scripture. It is clarified and confirmed as always being the basis of acceptance with God, in Romans 4. *Faith* is a matter not of merit, but of the readiness to accept what God promises.

***Faith* is a matter not of merit, but of the readiness to accept what God promises. Are you known as a person of this kind of *faith?* Explain.**

____

____

____

How long would you wait for God to fulfill His promise to you? Answer as honestly as possible.

❑ 1 MONTH ❑ 3 MONTHS

❑ 5 YEARS ❑ 10 YEARS

❑ 30 YEARS

- **Review what God has shown you through the lesson today.**
- **Look back over your lesson and take time to underline or highlight key statements that God used to impact your life.**
- **Write a statement here that God used most in your life today:**

____

____

____

- **Turn to the end of the chapter and write your statement again. This will provide a weekly list of key statements for you to meditate on the last two days of the week.**

  ❑ CHECK THIS BOX AFTER YOU HAVE DONE SO.
- **Take time to pray, asking God to adjust your life to how He has spoken to you today.**
- **With whom do you need to share this truth today?**

____

Summary Statements

- True faith persists until the promise is fulfilled. That is what makes it faith that pleases God!
- Delayed promises can diminish faith or strengthen faith!

DAY 5

Abram's Future

Faith is based not on a minimum of information, but on a maximum of information about God and His promises to us. This moment of saving *faith* did not come easily or quickly to Abram. He spent many years walking with God and would spend many more before God gave him a son. But Abram's *faith* had developed to the point where God would now entrust to him an intimacy given to no other person before this point in history.

***Faith* is based not on a minimum of information, but on a maximum of information about God and His promises to us.**

Do you have an intimate relationship with God that believes Him and waits for Him to do what He said? Explain your answer.

____

____

____

First, God affirmed that it was indeed He who had brought him out of Ur, to give him his land to inherit it. Second, God allowed Abram to question Him about how he would really know this was going to be true for him. Third, God asked a strange thing of him and revealed the future of his descendants. They would spend four hundred years in Egypt, mostly in captivity. God asked Abram to bring, and divide in two, a heifer, a goat, a ram, a pigeon, and a turtledove (the last two were not divided). In the dark of night, when Abram experienced "horror and great darkness," God spoke and "passed between those pieces" as God's *unique* Covenant with Abram (Gen. 15:12, 17). The Scripture then simply states,

> *On the same day the* LORD *made a covenant with Abram, saying . . .*
>
> **Genesis 15:18**

This awesome Covenant would be stated again, years later, at the birth of Isaac (Gen. 17).

A PERSONAL PROMISE FROM GOD

As a young man, a teenager, I began to pray that God would place on the hearts of my denomination a commitment to help bring the Gospel to my nation, Canada. From the beginning, God assured my heart that He had heard prayer (not only mine, but others'). I continued to pray and work and prepare my own life for God to use me. Years passed with my heart consistently crying out to God, for His promise to be fulfilled. A good, but partial answer came—thirty-two years later. My heart rejoiced. It was an additional twelve years later when I sat in our national conference and voted along with the others of my denomination when they finally "included Canada" as part of God's assignment for them. It had taken forty-four years to establish 135 churches and missions. Now we have adopted a goal of establishing 1,000 new churches and missions at the earliest possible moment.

This is special to me, for in 1972, one other coworker and I cried out to God for "1,000 churches in our group in Canada!" I could have confidence in God through all these years, for the God who fulfilled His promise to Abram after many, many years would be faithful to complete His promise to me and to my children.

Make a list of the promises God has made to you. After writing the list, make a notation by the promises that are prominent in your prayer life. Take time to renew in your mind and heart what God began.

Take time to remember your "spiritual conversion." Is there anything that has diminished in your life since then? If so, are you willing to take time

now to return to God in that area of your life? If not, explain what growth has taken place since your "spiritual conversion."

- Review what God has shown you through the lesson today.
- Look back over your lesson and take time to underline or highlight key statements that God used to impact your life.
- Write a statement here that God used most in your life today:

- Turn to the end of the chapter and write your statement again. This will provide a weekly list of key statements for you to meditate on the last two days of the week.

  ❑ CHECK THIS BOX AFTER YOU HAVE DONE SO.
- Take time to pray, asking God to adjust your life to how He has spoken to you today.
- With whom do you need to share this truth today?

SUMMARY STATEMENTS

- Faith is based not on a minimum of information, but on a maximum of information about God and His promises to us.

KEY STATEMENTS FOR MEDITATION

Day 1

Day 2

Day 3

Day 4

Day 5

UNIT 7

WRONG COUNSEL BRINGS TRAGIC CONSEQUENCES

Thought Starter

Trust in the L*ORD with all your heart,*
And lean not on your own understanding;
In all your ways acknowledge Him,
And He shall direct your paths.
Do not be wise in your own eyes;
Fear the L*ORD and depart from evil.*

PROVERBS 3:5–7

ELEVEN YEARS HAD PASSED since God made His initial Covenant with Abram. He still did not have a child, and the Promise of God seemed no closer. God had done wonderful things for Abram, and through these activities in his life, He had been steadily developing "His friend." Little did Abram know that God was developing the father to whom He could entrust His Isaac. For it was on Isaac, also, that the redemption of the world would rest. God could not trust just *any* father to Isaac! Character takes time to develop and establish.

Character takes time to develop and establish.

But sometimes it is the ones around us who grow impatient. They may not have had the same intensity of experience with God as we have had. They may begin to "interpret" the ways of God and make suggestions as to how we may be able "to help God out." But man's ways are never God's ways, no matter how sincerely they are presented. To substitute our ways of "helping God" for His ways of achieving His purpose is *Sin*. And *Sin* brings death to much in our lives, or affects our lives and the lives of others forever. This was to be Abram's experience.

To substitute our ways of "helping God" for His ways of achieving His purpose is *Sin.*

DAY 1

Wrong Thinking

Abram's wife, Sarai, suggested that they should follow an accepted custom of the world around them. They could have a child by the handmaid they had in their home. Besides, they were past childbearing years. God saw and heard, and did not intervene. Abram would have to learn *by experience* how serious *sin* was; he would also learn how deeply a covenant with God could affect others and history through his decisions. He would also know by experience the mercy and grace of God. The experience with God would affect his *faith* in God and make it possible thirteen years later to receive Isaac, and years beyond that to entrust Isaac back to God in sacrifice. In every circumstance of one chosen of God, God's very nature is that He is able to help us, even in our deepest sin.

> *Know that all things work together for good to those who love God, to those who are the called according to His purpose.*
>
> Romans 8:28

The Scripture merely records,

> *And Abram heeded the voice of Sarai.*
>
> Genesis 16:2

Take time to find Genesis 16 in your Bible. Read the entire chapter so you will have a good background for the counsel that Sarai gives. Record any key thoughts that God reveals to you as you read.

____

____

____

Sarai, though absolutely sincere, gave counsel—but not from God!

God had made His Covenant with Abram, and of course Sarai was included. But it seems that God left it to Abram to share extensively and adequately with Sarai all aspects of His Covenant. At this time probably ten years had passed.[1] During those years Abram and Sarai must have talked much about God's promises to them. It was the heart of Abram that God trusted. Sarai, though absolutely sincere, gave counsel—but not from God! It is obvious she believed a child could, and should, come from her husband, but she was not sure that

God could bring a child through her. She urged Abram to consider her reasoning, and Abram agreed. Still God did not intervene, even when He knew the severe consequences of this decision. God knew that Abram knew clearly the Covenant He had made. Abram *must* on his own keep his life clearly focused on God, especially when "different counsel" was given. This is especially true with a delayed promise. Abram lost his focus.

When Hagar, Sarai's handmaiden, conceived, sin began to work its work. Sarai's heart became greatly jealous, and she treated Hagar harshly. Hagar fled into the wilderness. In mercy God graciously visited her there, and made an eternal promise to her concerning her expected son. God would take part of His promise to Abram to "multiply your descendants exceedingly" and give it to Hagar and her son (Gen. 16:10). But because this child did not come from Him by *faith* on Abram's part, God also added,

> *He shall be a wild man;*
> *His hand shall be against every man,*
> *And every man's hand against him.*
>
> GENESIS 16:12[2]

Has sin brought awful consequences to your life? If so, have you repented? If not, why not do so now? Whether you have repented or not, write a story of the consequences sin brought to your life (much as David did in Psalm 38). Simply list the facts of what happened. Tomorrow you will have another assignment based on this story.

- **Review what God has shown you through the lesson today.**
- **Look back over your lesson and take time to underline or highlight key statements that God used to impact your life.**
- **Write a statement here that God used most in your life today:**

- **Turn to the end of the chapter and write your statement again. This will provide a weekly list of key statements for you to meditate on the last two days of the week.**

  ❑ CHECK THIS BOX AFTER YOU HAVE DONE SO.
- **Take time to pray, asking God to adjust your life to how He has spoken to you today.**
- **With whom do you need to share this truth today?**

SUMMARY STATEMENTS

- Character takes time to develop and establish.
- To substitute our ways of "helping God" for His ways of achieving His purpose is Sin.

DAY 2

REAPING WHAT YOU SOW

Sin is devastatingly real in its consequences in every person alike. There are no favorites or exceptions.

Sin carries awful consequences. Sin is devastatingly real in its consequences in every person alike. There are no favorites or exceptions. As great a man of *faith* as Abram was becoming, sin brought lasting consequences. Someone has said that because of the greatness of God, sin in His servants causes "great messes"! This was true with Abram. To the end of time, and in our own day, the consequences of Abram's sin at this moment in his life are being felt very powerfully. But God would again cause Abram to realize how significant his relationship to God was, on behalf of others. He revealed later to Abraham concerning Ishmael,

I will also make a nation of the son of the bondwoman, because he is your seed.

GENESIS 21:13 (EMPHASIS ADDED)

Based on the story you wrote yesterday, how did God use the consequences of sin to shape and mold your character?

____

____

____

____

____

____

____

____

____

____

____

____

____

____

____

Abram's self-effort to help God had far-reaching and tragic consequences. Sin always does! But Abram would increasingly take sin seriously. He was learning, with all God's interventions, to trust all God said and obey Him completely, regardless of "appearances" or the counsel of others, even those who were dearly loved!

Abram's self-effort to help God had far-reaching and tragic consequences. Sin always does!

"Godly" counsel is never a substitute for a word from God! God *may* use our friends to speak His word to us, but mere counsel from godly family or friends is never a safe substitute for a word from God and obedience to Him. And this danger often comes immediately to many following a call of God to mission work. Upon sharing God's call and claim on their lives to missions, people often are faced with family and friends who give their counsel against it, or at least suggest for them to wait or "do missions here at home." I have spoken with very special believers who heeded the counsel of their parents, or friends, and did not

"Godly" counsel is never a substitute for a word from God!

go to the mission field. Instead, they stayed home, took care of their parents, and lived with the consequences—which sometimes were significant.

God's counsel never gives wrong advice. What advice have you received from a friend that was not godly?

____

____

____

Have you ever given someone wrong advice? What could protect you from giving wrong advice?

____

____

____

- **Review what God has shown you through the lesson today.**
- **Look back over your lesson and take time to underline or highlight key statements that God used to impact your life.**
- **Write a statement here that God used most in your life today:**

____

____

____

- **Turn to the end of the chapter and write your statement again. This will provide a weekly list of key statements for you to meditate on the last two days of the week.**

  ❑ CHECK THIS BOX AFTER YOU HAVE DONE SO.
- **Take time to pray, asking God to adjust your life to how He has spoken to you today.**
- **With whom do you need to share this truth today?**

____

SUMMARY STATEMENTS

- Sin is devastatingly real in its consequences in every person alike. There are no favorites or exceptions.
- Self-effort to help God has far-reaching and tragic consequences. Sin always does!
- "Godly" counsel is never a substitute for a word from God!

DAY 3

Persistent Obedience

While it is true that some have refused to follow God, others have recovered, repented, and went on to the field and were greatly blessed of God, and their children carried on their commitment (as Abram's did). Others faced this counsel of the "flesh," saw it for what it was, and obeyed God immediately, even against the counsel of others.

What wrong choices have you made about which God was merciful and brought you back to correct your ways?

____

____

____

Others faced this counsel of the "flesh," saw it for what it was, and obeyed God immediately, even against the counsel of others.

Marilynn and I were sharing with a group of missionaries in East Africa. As the conference progressed the missionaries were given an opportunity to express themselves about their work. One veteran missionary, who had been on the mission field for years, expressed a real concern.

He said, "Here I am in Africa sharing God's message of salvation, yet neither of my parents is a Christian. My parents are aging. Should I go home and witness to them extensively so they can become Christians?"

He added, "They opposed our responding to God's call in our lives and did not even come to our commissioning service when we left many years ago. What should we do now?"

What advice would you give these missionaries?

____

____

____

____

____

____

God immediately guided me to suggest, first, that God had a greater concern for the salvation of his parents than he did, and that God was working in them to draw them to His Son; and second, that we should stop and surround the couple with this real burden, and pray with and for them.

This we did with great earnestness. The couple sensed a real peace and promised to let us know what happened next. We returned home to the U.S. In less than a month, we received a letter from this missionary. He wrote and told us that shortly after we prayed together he received word from his parents. They said they had suddenly felt the need to go down a country road to the nearby Baptist church. They did and, in their first worship service, heard the Gospel and received Jesus Christ into their lives as Lord. That next week they would be baptized into the fellowship of God's people. I could almost see the "tearstains" on the letter, expressing eternal joy for the goodness of God in rewarding their faith and obedience to Him over the years.

God is looking for the heart that is "loyal to Him" so He can "show Himself strong [on their behalf]" (2 Chron. 16:9). This moment in Abram's life is enormously instructive for us. The world waits to see what God can do through the life wholly yielded to God. This is especially true in our day. And I believe that one day, before God, He may let us see "what could have been done, if when He called, we obeyed." But from Abram's experience in the birth of Ishmael, never again can anyone say he does not realize what can happen when we follow the counsel of others as a substitute for God's counsel in our daily lives.

What accountability does it bring to your life to realize that one day, before God, He may let us see "what could have been done, if when He called, we obeyed"?

God may let us see "what could have been done, if when He called, we obeyed."

- **Review what God has shown you through the lesson today.**
- **Look back over your lesson and take time to underline or highlight key statements that God used to impact your life.**
- **Write a statement here that God used most in your life today:**

- **Turn to the end of the chapter and write your statement again. This will provide a weekly list of key statements for you to meditate on the last two days of the week.**

  ❑ CHECK THIS BOX AFTER YOU HAVE DONE SO.
- **Take time to pray, asking God to adjust your life to how He has spoken to you today.**
- **With whom do you need to share this truth today?**

____

SUMMARY STATEMENTS

- Persistent obedience will see the counsel of the "flesh" for what it is, and obey God immediately, even against the counsel of others.
- God may let us see "what could have been done, if when He called, we obeyed."

DAY 4

PREVENTION: REVIEW GOD'S PROMISES

In the midst of this enormous decision there is no mention that Abram reviewed with himself or with Sarai the original Covenant Promises of God! If he had returned with serious meditation to all God had said to him, believed God, and obeyed one more time, history may have been greatly different.

Take time to review what God has asked of you or what He has promised to you. Has there been a time when you knew you should have obeyed but did not? Is there a promise God gave you but you have lost sight of it? Write your answers here, and then take time to renew your Covenant with God.

____

____

____

____

____

Adam faced this same moment in his life. God had commanded him not to eat of the Tree of Good and Evil, or the Tree of Life. This was given to Adam before God gave Eve to him. He was to teach and instruct Eve. At a moment of "testing," Eve counseled Adam to eat, and he listened to her counsel—and sin entered the world with disastrous consequences.

Jesus also was tested (read Matt. 4). But He remembered Scripture, and remembered His Heavenly Father's commands, and turned aside from the temptation to disobey God. Salvation came through Him as a result of His unswerving obedience and faith.

Many people have thanked me for "my obedience" in writing *Experiencing God*, because their lives and churches have been greatly changed. I nearly always encourage them to ask, "And what could God do if you are obedient?"

Jesus remembered Scripture, and remembered His Heavenly Father's commands, and turned aside from the temptation to disobey God.

What can God do through your obedience?

- **Review what God has shown you through the lesson today.**
- **Look back over your lesson and take time to underline or highlight key statements that God used to impact your life.**
- **Write a statement here that God used most in your life today:**

- **Turn to the end of the chapter and write your statement again. This will provide a weekly list of key statements for you to meditate on the last two days of the week.**

  ❑ CHECK THIS BOX AFTER YOU HAVE DONE SO.
- **Take time to pray, asking God to adjust your life to how He has spoken to you today.**
- **With whom do you need to share this truth today?**

SUMMARY STATEMENTS

- Prevention of sin is found in obedience to God.
- Jesus remembered Scripture, and remembered His Heavenly Father's commands, and turned aside from the temptation to disobey God.

DAY 5

SIN IS ALWAYS AGAINST GOD

Abram's sin with Hagar was against God. Abram knew the Covenant with God, and ignored it under pressure. God makes no exceptions: "The soul who sins shall die" (Ezek. 18:4). Death began to work its way into Abram's life. Only the divine and merciful redemptive activity of God rescued him.

Only the divine and merciful redemptive activity of God rescued him.

David saw his sin as against God when he cried out:

Against You, You only, have I sinned,
And done this evil in Your sight.

PSALM 51:4

All sin is against God. How do we know that? If a person would stay in a right relationship to God as Jesus did, when temptation comes, he would turn toward God and not toward sin. David rightly remembered his relations with God, and added:

That You may be found just when You speak,
And blameless when You judge.

PSALM 51:4

David, like Abram, had a heart that was right with God and acknowledged:

> *Behold, You desire truth in the inward parts,*
> *And in the hidden part You will make me to know wisdom.*
>
> **PSALM 51:6**

Abram came to know by experience God in new ways—and responded carefully and acceptably with God. God's redeeming of Abram was quick and thorough. Abram did not argue with God, but believed Him and obeyed Him. Abram's character continued to be severely changed, and it pleased God to continue His Covenant with him.

Do you see your sin as "against God"? If so, have you truly repented toward God of your sin?

- **Review what God has shown you through the lesson today.**
- **Look back over your lesson and take time to underline or highlight key statements that God used to impact your life.**
- **Write a statement here that God used most in your life today:**

- **Turn to the end of the chapter and write your statement again. This will provide a weekly list of key statements for you to meditate on the last two days of the week.**

  ❑ CHECK THIS BOX AFTER YOU HAVE DONE SO.
- **Take time to pray, asking God to adjust your life to how He has spoken to you today.**
- **With whom do you need to share this truth today?**

Summary Statements

- All sin is against God.
- Only the divine and merciful redemptive activity of God can rescue you from sin.

KEY STATEMENTS FOR MEDITATION

Day 1

Day 2

Day 3

Day 4

Day 5

UNIT 8

A FRESH ENCOUNTER WITH GOD

Thought Starter

"No longer shall your name be called Abram, but your name shall be Abraham; for I have made you a father of many nations. I will make you exceedingly fruitful; and I will make nations of you, and kings shall come from you. And I will establish My covenant between Me and you and your descendants after you in their generations, for an everlasting covenant, to be God to you and your descendants after you. Also I give to you and your descendants after you the land in which you are a stranger, all the land of Canaan, as an everlasting possession; and I will be their God." And God said to Abraham: "As for you, you shall keep My covenant, you and your descendants after you throughout their generations."

Genesis 17:5–9

God watched the development of His "friend." He saw the changes in his heart. He knew Abram's character was being responsive to the Potter's Hand. For twenty-four years Abram was living under the shaping Hand of God. Abram was not the same man in character that he was when God first called him. Twenty-four years of close and intimate fellowship with God had changed him completely.

Throughout the Bible, when *character* changes significantly, God changes the name. In the economy of God, it was time for God to change Abram's name. He changed it from Abram ("exalted" or "high father") to Abraham ("father of a multitude" or "father of a multitude of nations").

This name change was essentially an announcement by God that God was now going to relate to him by his "new character"! God, by this name change, was announcing that He was now proceeding to touch the nations of the world through him. All God's activity would now move rapidly toward the ultimate purposes of God in His Covenant relation with Abraham.

DAY 1

A New Dimension of Life

But without faith it is impossible to please Him, for he who comes to God must believe that He is, and that He is a rewarder of those who diligently seek Him.

Hebrews 11:6

To the careful observer of history, it is obvious that the men and women God has mightily used throughout history have had a special moment of encounter with God, eleven to fifteen years or more into their ministry. This encounter issued in a different person. After this, God began to use them in ways mightier than in their entire previous ministries. More of God worked in them and through them than ever before. Was it a "name change"? Did God see the depth of their souls and their *faith* in Him that now He could trust them with greater blessings in their labors? I believe so!

I believe we can anticipate a relationship change with God that issues in a significant, measurable, observable difference in fruitfulness of our lives when we clearly let God shape our character over time. I say this because this name change is an essential aspect of God's shaping of the man He calls "His friend." You are seeing clearly a "pattern" in God's changing Abram's name to Abraham and later changing Jacob's name from Jacob ("trickster," "deceiver") to Israel ("Prince with God"; Gen. 32:27–28).

This same pattern is seen when Jesus changed Peter's name from Simon to Cephas or Peter (meaning "a stone"; John 1:42); and Saul the persecutor of believers met Jesus on the road to Damascus and was blinded by the Light (Acts 9:1–8), but when Ananias touched Saul in his blindness, Saul arose the Apostle of Jesus Christ (Acts 9:15–19).

With Abraham, God was shaping the man He would call "His friend." Centuries later, the writer James summed up this special moment: "Do you see that faith was working together with his works, and by works faith was made perfect? And the Scripture was fulfilled which says, 'Abraham believed God, and it was accounted to him for righteousness.' And he was called the friend of God" (James 2:22–23).

With God's changing Abram's name to Abraham, there begins a whole new dimension in his life.

For thirteen years Abram had "heard nothing from God." This never means that God is not actively at work. He is working His eternal purpose in you and around you. For Abram to hear nothing merely meant God had chosen not to let him know what He was doing. Even through God's silence a person can have specific occasions to *trust* Him. Again, *faith* is developed in real-life situations. "Sight" is not "faith." We constantly want God to "show us Your will for my life" even after He has assured us that He is doing just that. But God will do it in His way and in His time. We want to help God! He does not need *our* help; we need *His* help! The "silences" of God do not mean He is late, or inactive, or not working. It means that this is where *faith* works! We are to continue faithfully doing the last things that we heard from God, with confident expectation that in God's "fullness of time" He will speak and not delay. The prophet Habakkuk learned this truth at a time when the "silence" of God seemed unbearable to him. God finally did speak and said,

"Sight" is not "faith."

> *For the vision is yet for an appointed time;*
> *But at the end it will speak, and it will not lie.*
> *Though it tarries, wait for it;*
> *Because it will surely come,*
> *It will not tarry.*
>
> HABAKKUK 2:3

God's fresh encounter began with a fresh, new revealing of His Name (Himself). It is significant to realize that each additional revelation of God's Name follows a mighty act of God in the life of the individual or nation. Here, God (1) had just helped Abram defeat a powerful coalition of kings and (2) had just made a promise that seemed impossible to him—to give him a son by Sarai. So God said, "I am Almighty" (Gen. 17:1). Once God spoke this, or revealed this, what Abram did next would reveal what he believed about God. We must note, here, that we in our generation have the *Full* revelation, including His Son, Jesus Christ. There is no excuse for our unbelief or disobedience! We possess, in the Scriptures, the *Full* revelation, and have a much more significant understanding of God upon which to place our *faith* and *obedience*. Not only do we have the Scriptures but also two thousand years of history that bear witness to us of the faithfulness of God and the ways of God. Abram did not have near the knowledge that we have of God. Today, a life of *faith* and *obedience* is the only response worthy of the God who has revealed Himself to us so extensively!

Today, a life of *faith* and *obedience* is the only response worthy of the God who has revealed Himself to us so extensively!

We possess, in the Scriptures, the Full revelation, and have a much more significant understanding of God upon which to place our faith and obedience. Why do you think many Christians have "little faith"?

For Abram, to know God revealed as Almighty meant nothing would be impossible to Him. What He says from now on to Abram, God, who is Almighty, can Himself bring to pass, no matter how impossible to us. Abram was now being trusted with more of God than God had ever entrusted to others. But this was God's eternal plan from the beginning. We are seeing it unfold in a godly man's life. God then added, "Walk before Me and be blameless" (Gen. 17:1), and again added a promise,

> *And I will make* My *covenant between* Me *and you, and will multiply you exceedingly.*
>
> GENESIS 17:2

God was shaping Abram in his *heart*. God was personal, intimate, real—as a man talks to his "friend" (cf. Moses, too, in Ex. 33:11).

This is always God's pattern: He chooses, He calls, and He shapes a person in an intimate and loving relationship. God reveals Himself and His ways to the one He can trust. God's revelation is not for observation but to enable obedience! It takes time with God, but it also takes a daily, consistent walk of *faith* and *obedience*. For twenty-four years, Abram had walked faithfully with God, and God had so changed his heart that he could now change his name to match his changed character and God's implementing in him His promise.

God reveals Himself and His ways to the one He can trust.

God's revelation is not for observation but to enable obedience!

How did God choose, call, and shape you to have an intimate and loving relationship with Him?

God reveals Himself and His ways to the one He can trust. How much can God trust you?

God's revelation is not for observation but to enable obedience! Are you obedient to God in every area of your life right now? Explain.

- Review what God has shown you through the lesson today.
- Look back over your lesson and take time to underline or highlight key statements that God used to impact your life.
- Write a statement here that God used most in your life today:

- Turn to the end of the chapter and write your statement again. This will provide a weekly list of key statements to meditate on for the last two days of the week.

  ❑ CHECK THIS BOX AFTER YOU HAVE DONE SO.
- Take time to pray asking God to adjust your life to how He has spoken to you today.
- With whom do you need to share this truth today?

Summary Statements

- "Sight" is not "faith."
- Today, a life of faith and obedience is the only response worthy of the God who has revealed Himself to us so extensively!
- God reveals Himself and His ways to the one He can trust.
- God's revelation is not for observation but to enable obedience!

DAY 2

Heart Rebellion

There was no hint of rebellion in Abram's heart. He might have used bad judgment, and he might have failed in the midst of changing circumstances to seek a word from God, but there was no sense that in doing so he was deliberately going against the will of God. He was letting God guide him, develop him, and work in and through him. He was indeed walking "blameless" before God (in God's sight). He was living his life in the conscious Presence of God. He had made himself a servant of God, by a conscious choice, and was living under that accountability. When God directed him, he obeyed immediately. When God corrected or disciplined him, he accepted it as an expression of a loving relationship with God. He was responding to God as His "friend." Abram asked questions of God, but without a spirit of rebellion. Although he had many occasions when he *could* have argued with God, or resisted His directives, he did not! He had set his heart to love and serve God. This positioned both him and his family to be blessed of God. In fact, Abram was "keeping Covenant" with God.

Too many of God's people, especially His servants, fail to relate to God as His servants. When God is silent, they get upset or even angry at God. They begin to make demands of God, and too often forsake that last word from God. Others have a motto, similar to King Saul, "Don't just stand there; do something!" Using human reasoning, they create their own vision, proceed, and ask God to "bless them"! You never have to ask God to bless you—it is part of His Covenant with us!

You never have to ask God to bless you—it is part of His Covenant with us!

You never have to ask God to bless you—it is part of His Covenant with you! How is God blessing you and your family and friends?

When God can trust you with it, He will automatically bless you. His blessings will never be late or short. They will always be an expression of perfect love from God who is Almighty! Love never withholds anything when it is appropriate. Love longs to give and dispense. It is us who fail to appropriate what love has so consistently provided. One of the clearest and saddest moments in Israel's history that illustrates this truth is in Psalm 106:13–15:

> *They soon forgot His works;*
> *They did not wait for His counsel,*
> *But lusted exceedingly in the wilderness,*
> *And tested God in the desert.*
> *And He gave them their request,*
> *But sent leanness into their soul.*

It is very serious with God not to trust Him, and therefore wait on Him and obey Him. When one believes God, God "accounts it to him for righteousness." This is precisely what Abram was doing in his walk with God.

All too often God's people—and too often His spiritual leaders—do not obey God in *faith.* His people should believe that He has revealed Himself to us and will always be to us faithfully everything He has said. He would have to cease to be God to act toward us in a way contrary to His nature. I have seen this moment all too often in the lives of God's people. Know that God has promised in His Word, through the testimony of the Apostle Paul,

> *My God shall supply all your need according to His riches in glory by Christ Jesus.*
>
> PHILIPPIANS 4:19

Too many do not believe God for real-life situations. Add to this promise other promises such as the following:

> *And God is able to make all grace abound toward you, that you, always having all sufficiency in all things, may have an abundance for every good work.*
>
> 2 CORINTHIANS 9:8

His divine power has given to us all things that pertain to life and godliness, through the knowledge of Him who called us by glory and virtue, by which have been given to us exceedingly great and precious promises, that through these you may be partakers of the divine nature, having escaped the corruption that is in the world through lust.

2 PETER 1:3–4

These and a thousand more truths are ours to be appropriated, believed, received, and lived out in our daily lives. Yet I have watched many that would say, "I guess I just don't have that kind of *faith*!" They leave their situation and return to a comfortable and secure place for ministry. But they never know what God could and would have done for them had they just trusted Him. They never grew in their *faith* and usefulness to God. They forgot that God would have to cease to be God for Him to be unfaithful to one of His children with one of His promises. *Faith* can be lived out only in real, present situations. *Faith* is obvious in our lives when we are confronted with an opportunity to believe God and we obey Him immediately.

***Faith* is obvious in our lives when we are confronted with an opportunity to believe God and we obey Him immediately.**

- **Review what God has shown you through the lesson today.**
- **Look back over your lesson and take time to underline or highlight key statements that God used to impact your life.**
- **Write a statement here that God used most in your life today:**

____

____

____

____

- **Turn to the end of the chapter and write your statement again. This will provide a weekly list of key statements for you to meditate on the last two days of the week.**

  ❑ CHECK THIS BOX AFTER YOU HAVE DONE SO.
- **Take time to pray, asking God to adjust your life to how He has spoken to you today.**
- **With whom do you need to share this truth today?**

____

Summary Statements

- You never have to ask God to bless you—it is part of His Covenant with us!
- Faith is obvious in our lives when we are confronted with an opportunity to believe God and we obey Him immediately.

DAY 3

Family Impact

Too many do not realize another aspect of our *faith-obedience*—the impact and influence of our *faith* on the family, especially our children. Earlier I shared about our move from southern California to Saskatoon, Saskatchewan, Canada, to a church that wanted to disband. Our children watched us move through that process. There was no money to move us or to support us. All we had was a clear call from God. They saw why God asked us to move there and how God so faithfully met all our needs—one day at a time. They then saw God build His church to be a catalyst to see thirty-eight additional churches start and more than one hundred respond to God's call into ministry or missions and a theological college begin in their church.

Years later, one of my children was pastoring a church in Texas. One evening he called us and said, "Three churches in Canada called us tonight to see if we would be willing to come and be their pastor. Two are well-established churches, growing in number and secure in finances. The other is deciding whether to disband, having part of their facilities rented out to help pay the mortgage, and they have little money to move us or to pay us!"

I carefully asked, "And which of these three do you sense God would have you accept to be their pastor?"

I waited for his answer.

He said, "Guess!"

Then he added, "We've accepted the broken, discouraged little church because we saw what you and Mom did and how God blessed you!"

Obedience in Abram deeply affected his family after him, especially for God's eternal purpose through them. Even the prophet Malachi affirmed this when he spoke of the sacredness of marriage and said, "He [God] seeks godly offspring . . . Therefore take heed to your spirit" (Mal. 2:15).

Obedience in Abram deeply affected his family after him, especially for God's eternal purpose through them.

Little did Abram know what God was about to do in his life. But he knew

Worship is a *spontaneous* response to God's Presence.

God well enough that when God revealed His Name to him, he "fell on his face" (Gen. 17:3). Worship is a *spontaneous* response to God's Presence. What a person does *spontaneously* in God's Presence indicates the true condition of his heart toward God. The response of God to such heart-worship is overwhelming and immediate.

Describe the quality of your worship.

____

____

____

What a person does spontaneously in God's Presence indicates the true condition of his heart toward God.

God talked with him, saying:

> *"As for Me, behold, My covenant is with you, and you shall be a father of many nations. No longer shall your name be called Abram, but your name shall be Abraham; for I have made you a father of many nations. I will make you exceedingly fruitful; and I will make nations of you, and kings shall come from you. And I will establish My covenant between Me and you and your descendants after you in their generations, for an everlasting covenant, to be God to you and your descendants after you. Also I give to you and your descendants after you the land in which you are a stranger, all the land of Canaan, as an everlasting possession; and I will be their God."*
>
> **GENESIS 17:3–8**

Because Abram had responded faithfully over twenty-four years, God changed his name to match his character. This was an exceedingly special moment in God's dealings with Abraham. The intimacy and the "friendship" intensified, and God moved to complete His eternal purpose for Abraham. God would now give an outward sign of the completeness of the Covenant.

- **Review what God has shown you through the lesson today.**
- **Look back over your lesson and take time to underline or highlight key statements that God used to impact your life.**
- **Write a statement here that God used most in your life today:**

____

____

____

- **Turn to the end of the chapter and write your statement again. This will provide a weekly list of key statements for you to meditate on the last two days of the week.**

  ❑ CHECK THIS BOX AFTER YOU HAVE DONE SO.
- **Take time to pray, asking God to adjust your life to how He has spoken to you today.**
- **With whom do you need to share this truth today?**

SUMMARY STATEMENTS

- Worship is a spontaneous response to God's Presence.
- What a person does spontaneously in God's Presence indicates the true condition of his heart toward God.
- Obedience deeply affects your family, especially for God's eternal purpose through them.

DAY 4

A SPECIAL SIGN FOR HIS COVENANT

With Abraham, God's sign of Covenant was to be circumcision. In the New Testament, the Covenant sign is believer's baptism. This would be a sign, both to God's people and to the world, of an intimate relationship of commitment and *faith* with God—a Covenant relationship with God. This step of *faith* would not be taken lightly, but very seriously. This sign would separate God's people from the world around them. Circumcision would signify that they were "God's special possession"! He would be their God, and they would be His people. And both they and the world around them would know this difference. The difference would be seen (1) in the way Abraham and his descendants would respond to God—being holy and obedient to all His commands, statutes, and laws; and (2) in the way God would respond to His people—He would bless them, multiply them, and treat them as His "special treasure," above all the peoples of the earth. The Scriptures state:

> *"Now therefore, if you will indeed obey My voice and keep My covenant, then you shall be a special treasure to Me above all people;*

for all the earth is Mine. And you shall be to Me a kingdom of priests and a holy nation." These are the words which you shall speak to the children of Israel.

EXODUS 19:5–6

But you are a chosen generation, a royal priesthood, a holy nation, His own special people, that you may proclaim the praises of Him who called you out of darkness into His marvelous light; who once were not a people but are now the people of God, who had not obtained mercy but now have obtained mercy.

1 PETER 2:9–10

It is the nature of *faith* to be accompanied by a life lived consistently and obediently with God.

God told Abraham, "My covenant shall be in your flesh for an everlasting covenant" (Gen. 17:13). It is the nature of *faith* to be accompanied by a life lived consistently and obediently with God. James made it clear that "faith without works is dead" (James 2:26). The "works" confirm that the *faith* is truly the *faith* that is acceptable to God and now sealed by a "sign" given to them by God.

Since it is the nature of faith to be accompanied by a life lived consistently and obediently with God, how could you improve the sharing of your faithful life with God toward those around you?

____

____

____

Immediate *obedience,* even when this is a strange and painful command, is the hallmark of godly *faith*!

There was no hesitation! First, immediate *obedience*, even when this is a strange and painful command, is the hallmark of godly *faith*! This is precisely what God had been shaping in Abraham over twenty-four years. This is the kind of *faith* that God "accounts for righteousness" (Gen. 15:6; Rom. 4:3, 9, 22–23). And second, Abraham's obedience was thorough—it included himself, Ishmael, and his entire household (Gen. 17:23–27).

Immediate obedience, even when this is a strange and painful command, is the hallmark of godly faith! Is there any area of your life in which you are struggling to obey? If so, what will you do next?

____

____

____

- **Review what God has shown you through the lesson today.**
- **Look back over your lesson and take time to underline or highlight key statements that God used to impact your life.**
- **Write a statement here that God used most in your life today:**

- **Turn to the end of the chapter and write your statement again. This will provide a weekly list of key statements for you to meditate on the last two days of the week.**

  ❑ CHECK THIS BOX AFTER YOU HAVE DONE SO.
- **Take time to pray, asking God to adjust your life to how He has spoken to you today.**
- **With whom do you need to share this truth today?**

SUMMARY STATEMENTS

- It is the nature of faith to be accompanied by a life lived consistently and obediently with God.
- Immediate obedience, even when this is a strange and painful command, is the hallmark of godly faith!

DAY 5

IMMEDIATE FAITH

These two truths need to be expanded for better understanding of the response God is looking for in our lives today.

First, Abraham's obedience was *immediate*! The Scriptures indicate "that very same day, as God had said to him" (Gen. 17:23), Abraham and his entire household were circumcised. In addition, because of this new dimension of God's Covenant with Abraham, Sarai's name was changed. Sarai (some suggest this meant "contentious" while others say it is another form of Sarah) would now become Sarah ("princess"), and as He had done for Abraham, God promised, "I will bless her, and she shall be a mother of nations; kings of peoples shall be from her" (Gen. 17:16). Abraham's *faith* clearly affected deeply the life of his wife. It always does!

Second, what God was doing with Abraham because of his *faith,* God also brought to Abraham's wife. It cannot be stressed enough that the "ways of God" include the blessing of others around the life of *faith* that pleases God. In my life right now I see that what He is doing in and through me is being seen in my family. I have had the joy of speaking extensively to God's people. My wife and my children are experiencing that privilege. I have been privileged to write books. Now some of my sons are writing, and my wife and other sons and daughter are looking to that privilege also. So much has come to my family as I have sought earnestly to be faithful to God and walk with Him in absolute integrity.

The "ways of God" include the blessing of others around the life of *faith* that pleases God.

However, by now, Abraham had developed an intimate love of his "first" son, Ishmael. Therefore, he sought a blessing for this son and cried out,

"Oh, that Ishmael might live before You!"

GENESIS 17:18

God patiently and lovingly knew Abraham's heart, and assured him that it would be from Sarah that the son of promise would come "at this set time next year" (Gen. 17:21)—in God's "fullness of time." God is God, and Abraham was not! God knew this, and now Abraham knew this. It was settled!

When I was just a little boy, God convinced me that He is God, and I am not! This realization shaped the rest of my life. I have never entered His Presence without this strong awareness. So I cannot remember arguing with God, or demanding of God, or doubting God. I cannot remember fussing with God, or debating with God. He is God! And I am not! Therefore, I choose to let Him *be* God in and through my life. I constantly stand amazed at God's consistent blessing in my life and in my family!

This means that at every point in my life I have only one decision to make: Is this clearly God's will? If it is, I confirm it with my wife and children, and then proceed. There are always a hundred details to work out. But I am, and have always been, confident that since I know His will, each and all of these details He will work out or help me to work out in my life.

Many have said to me about their situation, "If these four things work out, I will know it is God's will!" I try gently to suggest that if this is God's will, those four things will work out! The key is God, not circumstances. Abraham was learning this one day and one circumstance at a time.

How have you known God's will in your life?

At every point in life you have only one decision to make: Is this clearly God's will? How would you know clearly that it is God's will?

- Review what God has shown you through the lesson today.
- Look back over your lesson and take time to underline or highlight key statements that God used to impact your life.
- Write a statement here that God used most in your life today:

- Turn to the end of the chapter and write your statement again. This will provide a weekly list of key statements for you to meditate on the last two days of the week.
  ❑ CHECK THIS BOX AFTER YOU HAVE DONE SO.
- Take time to pray, asking God to adjust your life to how He has spoken to you today.
- With whom do you need to share this truth today?

SUMMARY STATEMENTS

- True faith obeys immediately.
- The "ways of God" include the blessing of others around the life of faith that pleases God.

KEY STATEMENTS FOR MEDITATION

Day 1

Day 2

Day 3

Day 4

Day 5

UNIT 9

FAITH THROUGH DIFFICULTIES

Thought Starter

And the LORD said, "Shall I hide from Abraham what I am doing, since Abraham shall surely become a great and mighty nation, and all the nations of the earth shall be blessed in him? For I have known him, in order that he may command his children and his household after him, that they keep the way of the LORD, to do righteousness and justice, that the LORD may bring to Abraham what He has spoken to him."

GENESIS 18:17–19

ABRAHAM NOW HAD A NEW NAME and thus a new relationship of trust with God. Abraham would now face an entirely new relationship with the Heart of God. He was now forever "on mission with God" in his world! God had never before shared with Abraham any of the significant activities of God in the world.

But now God was to reveal what He was seeing and planning to do against Sodom and Gomorrah. God said that "the outcry against Sodom and Gomorrah is great, and because their sin is very grave, I will go down now and see" (Gen. 18:20–21). As God proceeded toward Sodom to destroy it, He again stopped to strategically affirm to Abraham and Sarah that they would have a son, in God's appointed time. Sarah overheard this and laughed.

God, in His infinite mercy, merely said, "Is anything too hard for the LORD?" (Gen. 18:14). This statement would deeply affect Abraham once again. This moment would be strategic in its timing for him. He would again face what to man was impossible, when God revealed to him His purpose toward Sodom and Gomorrah. To be a "friend" of God means to share His Heart—especially at the moments of His judgment. This is why later Jeremiah was called a "weeping prophet"—because he was permitted by God to know His Heart toward His people. It was a time of utter judgment! And Jeremiah almost could not contain his sorrow, once he knew, and asked to be relieved of his "assignment" as a prophet.

To be a "friend" of God means to share His Heart—especially at the moments of His judgment.

DAY 1

The Shaping Process

This growing intimacy of the "friend" of God with the Heart of God is seen clearly when God seems to be conversing in heaven and says,

> *Shall I hide from Abraham what I am doing, since Abraham shall surely become a great and mighty nation, and all the nations of the earth shall be blessed in him?*
>
> **Genesis 18:17–18**

The Potter was continuing to shape the clay into a strong person of *faith.* But his *faith* would be expanded and tested in new and significant ways. He would be given the opportunity to be an intercessor before God. God always looked for someone "who would make a wall, and stand in the gap before Me on behalf of the land, that I should not destroy it" (Ezek. 22:30). So God revealed to Abraham the imminent danger of these two cities. Now the "shaping" continued! What would Abraham do with this new information that had been given to him?

Make a list of the things you believe a friendship with God brings out in a person.

____

____

____

____

It is a moment of trembling to realize the Heart of God, but this comes to the one who chooses to let God draw him closer to Himself.

The men turned and went toward Sodom, "but Abraham still stood before the LORD. And Abraham came near and said, 'Would You also destroy the righteous with the wicked?'" (Gen. 18:22–23). Only a "friend of God" would approach Him with such boldness and openness! But God had been shaping him for such a time as this! What would Abraham, "His friend," do when he heard God in this matter? Abraham began to intensely intercede! This is the kind of *faith* that God had purposed from eternity. It was now real and personal in Abraham. God wanted someone with heart to stand before Him and intercede!

It is a moment of trembling to realize the Heart of God, but this comes to the one who chooses to let God draw him closer to Himself. Often this will occur in one, while others around him do not know anything at all about the seriousness of the moment with God. But God desires such a relationship, where He can share His Heart. This is the "friend" He is looking for. This is the kind of relationship He is shaping in the one He calls. This one will see farther, see clearer, and see more than others around him. This, too, will often separate him from those around him, especially because of the intensity with God this revelation creates. It is sometimes lonely being a "friend of God"!

The one God calls will see farther, see clearer, and see more than others around him.

To walk faithfully with God will always bring a person to experience God's laying His Heart over his. This moment had now come to Abraham. This moment came to Moses when God was about to deliver His people out of Egypt's agonizing bondage. From that crucial moment until later, Moses would experience many, many times the Heart of God. God's Heart was laid bare to both Abraham and Moses, and it always deeply affected them. Much later the disciples of Jesus would share His Heart, especially Peter, James, and John in Gethsemane (Matt. 26:36–46). But here, for the first time, Abraham was exposed, by God's Sovereign choice, to what was on God's Heart and God's agenda. It was awesome! And it always is!

To walk faithfully with God will always bring a person to experience God's laying His Heart over his. Have you reached that point in your relationship with God?

____

____

____

____

To walk faithfully with God will always bring a person to experience God's laying His Heart over his.

Amos knew this and cried out, "Surely the Lord GOD does nothing, unless He reveals His secret to His servants the prophets" (Amos 3:7). And Amos, like Abraham, was immediately caught up with God on mission to Israel, His people.

This was a new experience for Abraham, granted to him by God. God's decision to let him know His will was based firmly on God's Covenant with Abraham, and his new and trusted relationship with God. It should be noted that this kind of intimate relationship with God would be passed on to Abraham's descendants, even to this very day.

- **Review what God has shown you through the lesson today.**
- **Look back over your lesson and take time to underline or highlight key statements that God used to impact your life.**

- **Write a statement here that God used most in your life today:**

____

____

____

- **Turn to the end of the chapter and write your statement again. This will provide a weekly list of key statements for you to meditate on the last two days of the week.**

  ❑ CHECK THIS BOX AFTER YOU HAVE DONE SO.
- **Take time to pray, asking God to adjust your life to how He has spoken to you today.**
- **With whom do you need to share this truth today?**

____

SUMMARY STATEMENTS

- It is a moment of trembling to realize the Heart of God, but this comes to the one who chooses to let God draw him closer to Himself.
- The one God calls will see farther, see clearer, and see more than others around him.
- To walk faithfully with God will always bring a person to experience God's laying His Heart over his.

DAY 2

INSIGHTS FROM GOD

The closer one comes in his relationship with God, the more immediate is the intercession when the Heart of God is revealed to him.

The closer one comes in his relationship with God, the more immediate is the intercession when the Heart of God is revealed to him. This is a sure test of one's intimacy with God! Delay can be fatal!

It has been eternally true that "the Lord is . . . not willing that any should perish but that all should come to repentance" (2 Peter 3:9). So anyone close to God will by that relationship become an intercessor before God. This is what happened to Abraham; he immediately pleaded before God for the city.

He was especially concerned about his family. Lot and his family were in immediate danger! He continued reasoning with God, and astonishingly, for the first time in history, God responded to Abraham's clear and specific intercession. God was moved and pleased with Abraham, "His friend"! He knew God's Heart and responded to what he knew of God, until the Scriptures simply say,

> *So the Lord went His way as soon as He had finished speaking with Abraham; and Abraham returned to his place.*
>
> GENESIS 18:33

What a moment in history! What a pattern for all time! A "friend of God" being granted an insight into the Heart of God and becoming a "worker together with God" (1 Cor. 3:9; 2 Cor. 6:1). And it seems that the highest mission with God is intercession. Even to this moment, our Lord's activity in heaven is intercession!

It seems that the highest mission with God is intercession.

> *Who is he who condemns? It is Christ who died, and furthermore is also risen, who is even at the right hand of God, who also makes intercession for us.*
>
> ROMANS 8:34

> *Therefore He is also able to save to the uttermost those who come to God through Him, since He always lives to make intercession for them.*
>
> HEBREWS 7:25

Since this is the high ministry of our risen Lord today, any intimate relationship with Him will ultimately lead one to intercession, life-and-death intercession as well. That is what being a "friend of God" is all about!

- **Review what God has shown you through the lesson today.**
- **Look back over your lesson and take time to underline or highlight key statements that God used to impact your life.**
- **Write a statement here that God used most in your life today:**

____

____

____

- **Turn to the end of the chapter and write your statement again. This will provide a weekly list of key statements for you to meditate on the last two days of the week.**

  ❑ CHECK THIS BOX AFTER YOU HAVE DONE SO.
- **Take time to pray, asking God to adjust your life to how He has spoken to you today.**
- **With whom do you need to share this truth today?**

SUMMARY STATEMENTS

- The closer one comes in his relationship with God, the more immediate is the intercession when the Heart of God is revealed to him.
- It seems that the highest mission with God is intercession.

DAY 3

STANDING FOR OTHERS

Here I stand on holy ground and with great fear and trembling share some of my own heart. This has been my testimony now for forty years of ministry. The closer one comes to God in a love-relationship, the more God develops an immediate life of intercession. Only a confident *faith* in God will bring a child of God to such boldness in the Presence of God. But knowing He is the One who has brought you this far, you respond, "Yes, Lord!"

Only a confident *faith* in God will bring a child of God to such boldness in the Presence of God.

After reading the following Scripture, answer this question: "How does your prayer life compare to the one represented in this Scripture?"

> *Seeing then that we have a great High Priest who has passed through the heavens, Jesus the Son of God, let us hold fast our confession. For we do not have a High Priest who cannot sympathize with our weaknesses, but was in all points tempted as we are, yet without sin. Let us therefore come boldly to the throne of grace, that we may obtain mercy and find grace to help in time of need.*
>
> HEBREWS 4:14–16

What area of your prayer life needs special attention?

As was the case with Abraham, such closeness to God will bring boldness before God in behalf of wayward family members, or families in great danger, even if they are unaware of it. You may be hundreds of miles away when God awakens you to danger that is imminent and yet unknown to family members. You stand before God on their behalf because of the Heart of God in you.

Our family has experienced this many times. One time stands out above others. Our three older boys were in university and had decided to go about four hundred miles west into the Rocky Mountains for a student retreat. It was a winter retreat. Before they started on the trip, my wife had a sudden uneasiness in her heart. She strongly urged the boys not to travel in the same car. Being boys, they laughed and said, "Which one of us do you not want to get killed?" She was insistent. Several days later, on a Sunday afternoon when we knew the boys would be traveling home, Marilynn again suddenly felt the overwhelming conviction that we must immediately pray for their safety. I was taking my Sunday afternoon nap. She woke me up and pulled me to my knees to pray for our boys! We did, earnestly, until we sensed peace from our Lord.

Later that day the boys returned and immediately said, "You will never guess what happened! We were driving home in the mountains and we hit black ice and our car began to spin out of control and into the path of an oncoming eighteen-wheeler truck. Suddenly, as if a Hand gripped us, our tires caught and took us across to the other side to safety."

Two of our boys were in that car. I asked them, "What time was it when this happened?" We found out it was exactly the time we were on our knees in prayer. We shared this with our boys and bowed and thanked God for His kindness. Oh, how grateful we were to be in the kind of relationship with God where He could alert us, and we would know it was Him and we could respond.

Those called to the mission fields of the world often develop such bold intercession. The atmosphere and circumstances of the mission field often are lived in a very close relationship with God. This closeness almost always develops, at the same time, a spontaneous life of intercession. This relationship is often very heavy and often painful. The missionary, like Abraham, sees and hears things from God not seen or heard by others. It is sometimes lonely to be "a friend of God"! The blessings are there, but also the pain, especially the pain of knowing the Heart of God toward the real world. In the midst of our world, what is God revealing to you? Is your walk with God moving in the arena of significant intercession, for specific information given to you from God? Are you still in a relationship with God where He is only your Friend? Could He, right now, call you "His friend"?

It is sometimes lonely to be "a friend of God"!

In the midst of our world, what is God revealing to you?

Is your walk with God moving in the arena of significant intercession, for specific information given to you from God?

Are you still in a relationship with God where He is only your Friend? Could He, right now, call you "His friend"?

- **Review what God has shown you through the lesson today.**
- **Look back over your lesson and take time to underline or highlight key statements that God used to impact your life.**
- **Write a statement here that God used most in your life today:**

- **Turn to the end of the chapter and write your statement again. This will provide a weekly list of key statements for you to meditate on the last two days of the week.**

  ❑ CHECK THIS BOX AFTER YOU HAVE DONE SO.
- **Take time to pray, asking God to adjust your life to how He has spoken to you today.**
- **With whom do you need to share this truth today?**

SUMMARY STATEMENTS

- Only a confident faith in God will bring a child of God to such boldness in the Presence of God.
- It is sometimes lonely to be "a friend of God!"

DAY 4

GOD IS YOUR LIFE

The story of the destruction of Sodom and Gomorrah, Abraham's intercession, and God's mercy in saving Lot and his two daughters is described in Genesis 18–19.

STOP AND READ GENESIS 18–19.

Abraham had been made aware that God was "Almighty." Now he saw a dimension of this that left him a changed person. It was crystal clear to Abraham that the "wages of sin is death" (Rom. 6:23). But he also came to know by experience that "the gift of God is eternal life." It was becoming evident to Abraham that a Covenant relationship with God was his very *life*! Any person in covenant with God sees things others do not; he hears things others do not hear; and his heart knows things others do not know. This is what Jesus said to His disciples in Matthew 13:11–17:

> *Because it has been given to you to know the mysteries of the kingdom of heaven, but to them it has not been given. For whoever has, to him more will be given, and he will have abundance; but whoever does not have, even what he has will be taken away from him. Therefore I speak to them in parables, because seeing they do not see, and hearing they do not hear, nor do they understand.*

Any person in covenant with God sees things others do not; he hears things others do not hear; and his heart knows things others do not know.

And in them the prophecy of Isaiah is fulfilled, which says:

> *"Hearing you will hear and shall not understand,*
> *And seeing you will see and not perceive;*
> *For the hearts of this people have grown dull.*
> *Their ears are hard of hearing,*
> *And their eyes they have closed,*
> *Lest they should see with their eyes and hear with their ears,*
> *Lest they should understand with their hearts and turn,*
> So that I should heal them."

But blessed are your eyes for they see, and your ears for they hear; for assuredly, I say to you that many prophets and righteous men desired to see what you see, and did not see it, and to hear what you hear, and did not hear it.

One cannot, today, go through this experience with Abraham, concerning Sodom and Gomorrah, without trembling before our Holy God. There is much that is learned about the *faith* that God "accounts for righteousness":

- The God we serve is Holy and Just, and takes sin seriously.
- To be God's servant brings with it awesome insight and revelation from God.
- Intercession accompanies intimacy with God.
- The *faith* that saves is a *faith* that is always "on mission with God in the world."
- God is absolutely sovereign in His dealings with men.
- Serious intercession before God prepares *us* for other moments requiring great *faith*.
- God enlists an intercessor; He does not ask for a volunteer.
- You will never be the same, in your relations with God, after a serious moment of intercession before a Holy God.

Serious intercession before God prepares *us* for other moments requiring great *faith.*

Do you have any sense of a growing intimacy with God? (Check all that apply.)

❑ Most of the time. ❑ Not in my prayer life.

❑ More today than ever before. ❑ No, I need to return to God.

❑ Yes, it is evident. ❑ Rarely.

Are you seeing things and hearing things and feeling things that others do not?

❑ Most of the time.	❑ Not in my prayer life.
❑ Yes, in my prayer life.	❑ No, I need to return to God.
❑ Yes, it is evident.	❑ Rarely.

And are you experiencing an increasing "pain" level in all this and a growing trembling in God's Presence?

❑ Most of the time.	❑ Not in my prayer life.
❑ More today than ever before.	❑ No, I need to return to God.
❑ Yes, it is evident.	❑ Rarely.

You can be most fortunate if you grow in your relationship to God. Stay close to God in the days to come, and do not be surprised at what God lets you know about His activity in your world.

- **Review what God has shown you through the lesson today.**
- **Look back over your lesson and take time to underline or highlight key statements that God used to impact your life.**
- **Write a statement here that God used most in your life today:**

____

____

____

____

____

____

- **Turn to the end of the chapter and write your statement again. This will provide a weekly list of key statements for you to meditate on the last two days of the week.**

  ❑ Check this box after you have done so.
- **Take time to pray, asking God to adjust your life to how He has spoken to you today.**
- **With whom do you need to share this truth today?**

____

Summary Statements

- The God we serve is Holy and Just, and takes sin seriously.
- To be God's servant brings with it awesome insight and revelation from God.
- Intercession accompanies intimacy with God.
- The faith that saves is a faith that is always "on mission with God in the world."
- God is absolutely Sovereign in His dealings with men.
- Serious intercession before God prepares us for other moments requiring great faith.
- God enlists an intercessor; He does not ask for a volunteer.
- You will never be the same, in your relations with God, after a serious moment of intercession before a Holy God.

DAY 5

God Protects His Servant

A character flaw does not mean God rejects a person. But often a character flaw repeated may be passed on to the following generations.

A character flaw does not mean God rejects a person. But often a character flaw *repeated* may be passed on to the following generations. God watched Abraham repeat his sin of deception, now with Abimelech, king of Gerar (Gen. 20). Abraham had deceived Pharaoh by telling him that Sarah was his sister, and thus put everyone in jeopardy. Abraham repeated this deception and lack of trust in God with Abimelech. It is very instructive to note again that God did not interrupt Abraham's decision, but let him proceed. But this time God again dramatically intervened:

> *God came to Abimelech in a dream by night, and said to him, "Indeed you are a dead man because of the woman whom you have taken, for she is a man's wife."*
>
> Genesis 20:3

What a solemn and frightening moment this was for the king. I must add that with so much adultery and divorce in our day, this ought to be just as serious a moment for anyone in our day who takes another man's wife! The king responded with utter horror and fear and rightly pleaded with God, saying, "In the integrity of my heart and innocence of my hands I have done this" (Gen. 20:5).

Is there a character flaw that keeps repeating in your life? If so, what is it, and what will you do next?

____

____

____

God's response is classic! God's response reveals so much about Him and Abraham's relationship with Him. First, He replied,

> *Yes, I know that you did this in the integrity of your heart.*
>
> GENESIS 20:6

Again, God always reads the heart and therefore deals with us according to the heart, even in a person of the world. Then, God added an incredible statement about His love and care of all persons, especially those who are "touching His Own"! God then spoke this life-changing truth: "For I also withheld you from sinning against Me; therefore I did not let you touch her" (Gen. 20:6). As God had stated in His Covenant with Abraham, anyone who touches him for any reason touches God Himself. God announced that to Abimelech, without Abraham even knowing how mercifully God was protecting him even in his sin.

But in His communication with the king, God announced two other vital truths. For the first time God mentioned a man being a prophet, one who speaks for God: "Now therefore, restore the man's wife; for he is a prophet" (Gen. 20:7).

What an affirmation, from God, of how He had shaped "His friend" Abraham. It is one thing to declare yourself to be a prophet. It is quite another for God to declare that you are. Abraham has come a long way with God for God to reveal to others what he had become in God's sight!

It is one thing to declare yourself to be a prophet. It is quite another for God to declare that you are.

God declared a second fact about "His friend" Abraham: "He will pray for you and you shall live. But if you do not restore her, know that you shall surely die, you and all who are yours" (Gen. 20:7). How crucial it was for God to prepare Abraham to be an intercessor before Him, when He told him about Sodom and Gomorrah. It was crucial for Abimelech and all who were his, and it was crucial for Abraham in his relationship with God. The fullest relationship with God calls for the fullest obedience! His life became "life and death"

The fullest relationship with God calls for the fullest obedience!

to others. God does not entrust this to anyone except the one who has let God shape his character so God can trust him.

Because Abraham was a "friend of God" and a servant of God, his was a very serious presence. This is what God said in the beginning He would do with Abraham. This experience for Abraham with Abimelech was life penetrating and would never be repeated again. But it must be noted that he must have shared it with Isaac, and Isaac with Jacob, for they repeated this sin of deception. God also restored each man fully in his weakness because he had inherited the promises made to Abraham.

What are your children or friends learning from your life?

____

____

____

Abraham was still weak and vulnerable to his own thinking. Instead of focusing on the word of God, he said, "Because *I thought* . . ." (Gen. 20:11, emphasis added). Again, decisions without a word from God almost cost the king and all his house their lives. Today, as in all of history, most of God's people do not live close enough to God to realize the terrible Presence they bring to others. This pattern of *faith* lived out by Abraham is true of all that walk this same way with God. James expressed it this way: "The prayer of a righteous man has great power in its effects" (James 5:16 RSV), and the Phillips translation says,

Today, as in all of history, most of God's people do not live close enough to God to realize the terrible Presence they bring to others.

Tremendous power is made available through a good man's earnest prayer.

Abraham learned that the life of *faith,* as God develops it, has a profound effect upon others. "So Abraham prayed to God; and God healed Abimelech, his wife, and his female servants. Then they bore children" (Gen. 20:17), and Abraham had a new and deeper understanding of who he was with God in his world.

- **Review what God has shown you through the lesson today.**
- **Look back over your lesson and take time to underline or highlight key statements that God used to impact your life.**
- **Write a statement here that God used most in your life today:**

____

____

____

- **Turn to the end of the chapter and write your statement again. This will provide a weekly list of key statements for you to meditate on the last two days of the week.**

  ❏ CHECK THIS BOX AFTER YOU HAVE DONE SO.
- **Take time to pray, asking God to adjust your life to how He has spoken to you today.**
- **With whom do you need to share this truth today?**

SUMMARY STATEMENTS

- A character flaw does not mean God rejects a person. But often a character flaw repeated may be passed on to the following generations.
- It is one thing to declare yourself to be a prophet. It is quite another for God to declare that you are.
- Today, as in all of history, most of God's people do not live close enough to God to realize the terrible Presence they bring to others.

KEY STATEMENTS FOR MEDITATION

Day 1

Day 2

Day 3

Day 4

Day 5

UNIT 10

GOD ENTRUSTS ISAAC TO TWO PREPARED PARENTS

THOUGHT STARTER

And the Scripture was fulfilled which says, "Abraham believed God, and it was accounted to him for righteousness." And he was called the friend of God.

JAMES 2:23

IT TOOK GOD TWENTY-FIVE YEARS to shape the man to whom He could entrust Isaac. Isaac's father was essential to Isaac's *faith.* And Isaac would inherit the promises made to his father, Abraham. But twenty-five years of walking by *faith* with God gave him many, many stories to tell to his son. He would delight in telling him everything, from the very beginning. This telling of their history was a strong characteristic of God's people and their culture. God commanded that the fathers (and mothers) instruct their children carefully, especially in all the mighty deeds of God.

It took God twenty-five years to shape the man to whom He could entrust Isaac.

DAY 1

The Mighty Deeds of God

Read very carefully the following Scriptures:

Hear, O Israel: The L*ORD our God, the* L*ORD is one! You shall love the* L*ORD your God with all your heart, with all your soul, and with all your strength.*

And these words which I command you today shall be in your heart. You shall teach them diligently to your children, and shall talk of them when you sit in your house, when you walk by the way, when you lie down, and when you rise up. You shall bind them as a sign on your hand, and they shall be as frontlets between your eyes. You shall write them on the doorposts of your house and on your gates.

So it shall be, when the L*ORD your God brings you into the land of which He swore to your fathers, to Abraham, Isaac, and Jacob, to give you large and beautiful cities which you did not build, houses full of all good things, which you did not fill, hewn-out wells which you did not dig, vineyards and olive trees which you did not plant—when you have eaten and are full—then beware, lest you forget the* L*ORD who brought you out of the land of Egypt, from the house of bondage. You shall fear the* L*ORD your God and serve Him, and shall take oaths in His name. You shall not go after other gods, the gods of the peoples who are all around you (for the* L*ORD your God is a jealous God among you), lest the anger of the* L*ORD your God be aroused against you and destroy you from the face of the earth. You shall not tempt the* L*ORD your God as you tempted Him in Massah.*

DEUTERONOMY 6:4–16

A Contemplation of Asaph.
Give ear, O my people, to my law;
Incline your ears to the words of my mouth.
I will open my mouth in a parable;
I will utter dark sayings of old,
Which we have heard and known,
And our fathers have told us.
We will not hide them from their children,

Telling to the generation to come the praises of the L*ORD*,
And His strength and His wonderful works that He has done.
For He established a testimony in Jacob,
And appointed a law in Israel,
Which He commanded our fathers,
That they should make them known to their children;
That the generation to come might know them,
The children who would be born,
That they may arise and declare them to their children,
That they may set their hope in God,
And not forget the works of God,
But keep His commandments;
And may not be like their fathers,
A stubborn and rebellious generation,
A generation that did not set its heart aright,
And whose spirit was not faithful to God.

PSALM 78:1–8

Without a strong reference point from the past activity of God, the new generation would make fatal mistakes. The darkest period in the history of God's chosen people came during the time of the Judges. This darkness and forsaking of the ways of God can be attributed to a generation that did not know the Lord:

When all that generation had been gathered to their fathers, another generation arose after them who did not know the L*ORD nor the work which He had done for Israel.*

JUDGES 2:10

The people of God are always just one generation away from forsaking God and returning to paganism and rebellion against God! This is fatal for them, though they do not know this because they do not know God or His standards for them.

The people of God are always just one generation away from forsaking God and returning to paganism and rebellion against God!

This truth came over me with great force as I began to raise our four boys and our daughter. I felt that if they were ever to be able to have hearts that God could speak to and call for His purposes, I was going to have to tell them all I knew of the mighty deeds of God—especially in the family history. I called our family's great moments with God—"spiritual markers"! There were times in our lives, like times in Abraham's life, when God did such a work in us that the moment significantly shaped the rest of our lives with God. We faithfully shared these "markers" with each of our children from the earliest days of their lives. There was a time when we were raising four teenage boys at the same time! We knew their teen and university years would test them. Long before these times we had lived out our heritage and taught them carefully.

One of my sons picked me up at the Dallas/Ft. Worth airport, for he was in seminary at Ft. Worth. While driving from the airport I noticed tears in his eyes, and I knew he wanted to share something very special with me. He finally said, "Dad, I don't think you and Mom know how close we boys came to falling!"

I replied, "I'm sure that was true."

He then added, "Dad, when we were right at the moment when we could have fallen, we thought of you and Mom, and our heritage, and we just couldn't do it!"

My heart welled up with gratitude to God for His goodness in causing us to believe Him and obey Him by telling our children of the nature of our God and the mighty deeds that He had done for us. Now it was keeping our children!

Have you shared your "spiritual markers" with your children, family, or friends? Whether you have or not, take time to list what they are so that your mind is refreshed with God's activity in your life.

____

____

____

____

____

____

- **Review what God has shown you through the lesson today.**
- **Look back over your lesson and take time to underline or highlight key statements that God used to impact your life.**
- **Write a statement here that God used most in your life today:**

____

____

____

- **Turn to the end of the chapter and write your statement again. This will provide a weekly list of key statements for you to meditate on the last two days of the week.**

  ❑ CHECK THIS BOX AFTER YOU HAVE DONE SO.
- **Take time to pray, asking God to adjust your life to how He has spoken to you today.**

- **With whom do you need to share this truth today?**

> **Summary Statements**
> - The people of God are always just one generation away from forsaking God and returning to paganism and rebellion against God!
> - Remembering the mighty deeds of God can keep you on the right path.

DAY 2

God Develops Character

> *And not being weak in faith, he did not consider his own body, already dead (since he was about a hundred years old), and the deadness of Sarah's womb. He did not waver at the promise of God through unbelief, but was strengthened in faith, giving glory to God, and being fully convinced that what He had promised He was also able to perform.*
>
> Romans 4:19–21

Too much is at stake for God to entrust eternal matters and consequences to an immature person of faith.

After twenty-five years, in God's "fullness of time," God gave to Abraham and Sarah His promised son. God is never "late"! But Abraham had to learn the "ways" of God as well as the Nature of God. This always takes *time*! God knows what it will take to develop the character of the one He would trust with eternal things. Too much is at stake for God to entrust eternal matters and consequences to an immature person of faith. Unbelief, in any area of life, can have untold consequences in the lives of others and in the purposes of God. Eternity is at stake! This is always serious with God. Whatever it takes for a child of His to develop an essential character that God can trust, God will do. When extensive time passes between a promise given and the receiving of God's promise, too many break off the relationship, or fail to continue and obey, or begin to make demands of God, and therefore cancel what God would have done.

Whatever it takes for a child of His to develop an essential character that God can trust, God will do.

God knows what it will take to develop the character of the one He would trust with eternal things. What will it take for God to develop you?

Too much is at stake for God to entrust eternal matters and consequences to an immature person of faith. That is why God is developing your character. What character is God working on in your life?

Unbelief, in any area of life, can have untold consequences in the lives of others and in the purposes of God. How has God strengthened your belief?

It is never that God *can't* do a mighty work, but that He chooses not to when the character is not in place! Isaiah had a word from God for His people that showed how their hearts kept them from the promises of God:

> *Behold, the LORD'S hand is not shortened,*
> *That it cannot save;*
> *Nor His ear heavy,*
> *That it cannot hear.*
> *But your iniquities have separated you from your God;*
> *And your sins have hidden His face from you,*
> *So that He will not hear.*
>
> **ISAIAH 59:1–2**

It is never that God can't do a mighty work, but that He chooses not to when the character is not in place! Give an example of God witholding His mighty work because your character was not ready.

____

____

____

____

____

It is never that God can't do a mighty work, but that He chooses not to when the character is not in place!

- Review what God has shown you through the lesson today.
- Look back over your lesson and take time to underline or highlight key statements that God used to impact your life.
- Write a statement here that God used most in your life today:

____

____

____

____

- Turn to the end of the chapter and write your statement again. This will provide a weekly list of key statements for you to meditate on the last two days of the week.

  ❑ CHECK THIS BOX AFTER YOU HAVE DONE SO.
- Take time to pray, asking God to adjust your life to how He has spoken to you today.
- With whom do you need to share this truth today?

____

SUMMARY STATEMENTS

- Too much is at stake for God to entrust eternal matters and consequences to an immature person of faith.
- Whatever it takes for a child of His to develop an essential character that God can trust, God will do.
- It is never that God can't do a mighty work, but that He chooses not to when the character is not in place!

DAY 3

God Works on the Heart

When character is not in place, God works on the heart.

When character is not in place, God works on the heart. The Scripture says of Jesus, "Now He did not do many mighty works there because of their unbelief" (Matt. 13:58). And Jesus Himself stated,

> *Because of your unbelief; for assuredly, I say to you, if you have faith as a mustard seed, you will say to this mountain, "Move from here to there," and it will move; and nothing will be impossible for you.*
>
> Matthew 17:20

When belief is present in the life of God's child, He is free to fulfill the promise just as God did with Abraham.

For Abraham the long-awaited child is born! The Promise is being fulfilled! The eternal purposes of God are moving forward! World redemption is closer to reality than ever before! All the details of God are significant! From God's perspective (as God sees it), He leaves many crucial reminders of our past walk with Him. Often they are God's gentle deterrents to future situations. This is what He does with Abraham! God instructs them to call their son Isaac—meaning "laughter," for both Abraham and Sarah laughed when God promised them a son (Gen. 17:17; 18:12–15). His name, Isaac, would be a constant reminder of their sin of unbelief.

His name, Isaac, would be a constant reminder of their sin of unbelief.

Every time they called him by name or saw him they would be reminded of how they both had laughed before God when He told them He would give them a son in their old age. God chose Isaac's name for great purposes of His own in Abraham's and Sarah's lives. God would place every possible deterrent to unbelief in their lives. This was now one of those deterrents. But God also knew that Isaac, their long-awaited son, would bring them much joy—and laughter! His name, Laughter, would characterize God's mercy and grace and love to them.

From God's perspective (as God sees it), He leaves many crucial reminders of our past walk with Him. Often they are God's gentle deterrents to future situations. What deterrents has God placed in your life?

____

____

____

How has God used these deterrents in your life to help other people?

Even Isaac's name would be a great encouragement for others to obey all God says, which would issue in "great joy." Preeminently Isaac would not only bring great joy, but also be a reminder to Abraham and Sarah, and all who would follow them, that *faith* and immediate *obedience* are what God is always looking for. This kind of a relationship with God would bring great Covenant blessing.

All who followed Abraham as God's Covenant people, and would believe God and obey Him in their day, God would account that saving *faith* as righteousness and fill them with His joy. Jesus stated it clearly to His disciples when He said,

> *As the Father loved Me, I also have loved you; abide in My love. If you keep [practice] My commandments, you will abide in My love, just as I have kept My Father's commandments and abide in His love. These things I have spoken to you, that My joy may remain in you, and that your joy may be full.*
>
> JOHN 15:9–11

- **Review what God has shown you through the lesson today.**
- **Look back over your lesson and take time to underline or highlight key statements that God used to impact your life.**
- **Write a statement here that God used most in your life today:**

- **Turn to the end of the chapter and write your statement again. This will provide a weekly list of key statements for you to meditate on the last two days of the week.**

  ❑ CHECK THIS BOX AFTER YOU HAVE DONE SO.
- **Take time to pray, asking God to adjust your life to how He has spoken to you today.**
- **With whom do you need to share this truth today?**

Summary Statements

- When character is not in place, God works on the heart.
- How God corrects you is a constant reminder of your sin of unbelief.

DAY 4

Potential Harm

What an incredible unity of truth there is throughout the entire Bible. What is real in Abraham's life by God's activity is true and real in all others who walk by *faith* as Abraham did. Paul illustrated this to the early church when he shared,

> *Therefore He who supplies the Spirit to you and works miracles among you, does He do it by the works of the law, or by the hearing of faith?—just as Abraham "believed God, and it was accounted to him for righteousness." Therefore know that only those who are of faith are sons of Abraham. And the Scripture, foreseeing that God would justify the Gentiles by faith, preached the gospel to Abraham beforehand, saying, "In you all the nations shall be blessed." So then those who are of faith are blessed with believing Abraham.*
>
> Galatians 3:5–9

Conflict in the home is incompatible with godly upbringing.

But in giving them His promised son, God had also to remove any "conflict" in the home in order to develop the character of Isaac. Therefore, God oversees the expulsion of Hagar and Ishmael (Gen. 21:8–20). This time the advice of Sarah to Abraham is good advice and approved of God. Conflict in the home is incompatible with godly upbringing.

Stop and take time to read the details of this encounter in Genesis 21:8–20 in your Bible. Highlight or underline key statements.

The Scripture records essential details, which, if missed or not meditated on, could bring ruin to us as we seek to follow God in our pilgrimage. The Scriptures record,

Sarah saw the son of Hagar the Egyptian, whom she had borne to Abraham, scoffing [laughing].

GENESIS 21:9

Three major potentially disruptive factors are seen in this verse. Three things could have a hurtful effect on the character of Isaac, and that could be tragic. First, the disruption of Hagar, "the Egyptian." The influence of Egypt, with its many pagan gods and practices, still deeply resided in Hagar. We know this because later she secured a wife for Ishmael from Egypt (Gen. 21:21). This Egyptian influence, very real in Hagar and Ishmael, would have had negative influences on the growing and developing Isaac. God had to remove this early and did so in having Sarah "cast out" Hagar and Ishmael (Gen. 21:10).

Second, the phrase describing Ishmael as "whom she had borne to Abraham." There were strong ties of tender love between Abraham and Ishmael. He had given the boy special attention and love for fourteen years (cf. Gen. 17:24–25). He had made a special plea before God to use Ishmael for his inheritance, because he loved him greatly (Gen. 17:18). For Ishmael to remain in his home would bring serious division in Abraham's heart. Therefore the undistracted attention God knew Abraham must give to raising Isaac as a man of *faith* was to be protected. God had to remove Ishmael early, to give Abraham an unchallenged love for Isaac. It was to be through Isaac that the Promise would be fulfilled.

The undistracted attention God knew Abraham must give to raising Isaac as a man of faith was to be protected. How is God focusing your attention on Him?

____

____

____

____

Third, Sarah saw Ishmael scoffing and laughing, probably at her new baby, Isaac. God can grant unusual discernment at crucial moments. I believe Sarah's response was out of discernment. Ishmael's attitude, fashioned by his mother, Hagar, was one of cynicism and jealousy. This could not remain in the home without affecting Isaac's character seriously. So God guided the removal of Hagar and Ishmael from Abraham's home. It would not be without pain, but God would give watchcare over them all—for Abraham's sake!

God can grant unusual discernment at crucial moments.

- Review what God has shown you through the lesson today.
- Look back over your lesson and take time to underline or highlight key statements that God used to impact your life.
- Write a statement here that God used most in your life today:

___

___

___

- Turn to the end of the chapter and write your statement again. This will provide a weekly list of key statements for you to meditate on the last two days of the week.

  ❑ CHECK THIS BOX AFTER YOU HAVE DONE SO.
- Take time to pray, asking God to adjust your life to how He has spoken to you today.
- With whom do you need to share this truth today?

___

SUMMARY STATEMENTS

- Conflict in the home is incompatible with godly upbringing.
- God can grant unusual discernment at crucial moments.

DAY 5

THE DIMENSION OF GOD'S LOVE

Abraham immediately experienced pain at God's instructions: "And the matter was very displeasing in Abraham's sight because of his son" (Gen. 21:11). Once again God had to intervene and assure Abraham that "in Isaac your seed shall be called" (Gen. 21:12). Though in great sorrow, Abraham believed God and obeyed. Could this giving up of his first son, Ishmael, be preparation for being asked to give up his son Isaac, later, when he was the same age as Ishmael was now? God always prepares us beforehand for the big moments of decision. But God being God also assured Abraham that He would make of Ishmael a great nation, "because he is your seed" (Gen. 21:13). Abraham increasingly realized how special he was to God and to others!

God always prepares us beforehand for the big moments of decision.

How is God preparing you for moments of decision?

What decisions are you facing right now?

Hagar and Ishmael also experienced pain, distress, bewilderment, and the fear of death. In the desert, fearing imminent death, Hagar separated from her son so she would not have to watch him die.

Probably recalling the love and teaching of Abraham about God, the lad cried out to God. While Hagar, the Egyptian, was weeping (Gen. 21:16), God heard the cry (prayer) of the lad, Ishmael, and promised Hagar she and the lad would live and God would make of him a great nation. Again, we notice clearly that others associated with the one God calls are greatly blessed because of the promise God makes him! Abraham may have learned how God saved the life of his firstborn, Ishmael, and later would have confidence if He had spared Ishmael, He surely would spare Isaac—somehow!

God holds as sacred *any* seed of Abraham (Gen. 21:13), so the God whom Hagar came to know earlier ("the-God-Who-Sees" [Gen. 16:13–14]) was with her now, and "saw her, and the lad Ishmael," and heard the lad's cry (Gen. 21:17–20).

From God's perspective, He was teaching Abraham the larger dimension of His love, which would eventually include "all the nations of the world" that would be blessed through him.

From the birth of the son of Promise, God increasingly reminds Abraham that His ultimate purpose has always been, "in your seed all the nations of the earth shall be blessed, because you have obeyed My voice" (Gen. 12:3; 18:18; 26:4; Acts 3:25). The "seed" (singular) would be Jesus. But the means would be Abraham and his descendants' *faith*!

God also let Abraham realize how far-reaching his influence had become. God had done it, and Abraham would come to know the details of God's original Covenant, as Abimelech and Phichol affirmed the God of Abraham by saying, "God is with you in all that you do" (Gen. 21:22).

By now God was causing the world around Abraham to know clearly that he was a special servant of God. They saw the evidence in all Abraham did! Everything he did, God blessed, and a watching world saw it convincingly. Later, even Satan acknowledged this in Job 1:6–10. This promise to bless was written into the Covenant God later made with the nation He created, promising to bless everything they put their hands to also (Deut. 28:1–14).

So Abimelech and Phichol then sought a blessing from Abraham, which he readily gave, and established peace between them. God had taken at least thirty-five to forty years to bring Abraham to this point in his life before Him. The *final test* of the kind of *faith* that God was looking for, to be the pattern of *faith* for all time, was ready to be undertaken.

- **Review what God has shown you through the lesson today.**
- **Look back over your lesson and take time to underline or highlight key statements that God used to impact your life.**
- **Write a statement here that God used most in your life today:**

____

____

____

- **Turn to the end of the chapter and write your statement again. This will provide a weekly list of key statements for you to meditate on the last two days of the week.**

  ❑ CHECK THIS BOX AFTER YOU HAVE DONE SO.
- **Take time to pray, asking God to adjust your life to how He has spoken to you today.**
- **With whom do you need to share this truth today?**

____

SUMMARY STATEMENTS

- God always prepares us beforehand for the big moments of decision.

KEY STATEMENTS FOR MEDITATION

Day 1

Day 2

Day 3

Day 4

Day 5

UNIT 11

THE MOMENT OF TRUTH

Thought Starter

By faith Abraham, when he was tested, offered up Isaac, and he who had received the promises offered up his only begotten son, of whom it was said, "In Isaac your seed shall be called," concluding that God was able to raise him up, even from the dead, from which he also received him in a figurative sense.

Hebrews 11:17–19

Eternity would hold its breath! Time would stand still! So much was resting on one man, whom God called "His friend"! God had chosen this moment in the life of Abraham to give him one final test: "After these things . . . God tested Abraham" (Gen. 22:1). God's refining process was about to be completed. God's test was not so much to prove Abraham, but to refine him. All impurities would be totally removed and pure *faith* would remain. Nothing less than pure *faith* would be sufficient; nothing less than the refining process would produce it; and God's refining process is thorough! What God would ask next would require a response of pure *faith*—the kind God was looking for and had worked probably forty years to bring about in Abraham.

This is God's moment, and we need to go slowly, deliberately, and carefully through it all. It must be run from God's Heart and through God's eyes. This moment will gather together forty years of the shaping of Abraham, especially his *faith*, or heart toward God. This moment will gather together all God had revealed of Himself and His ways. This moment will reveal the true heart of Abraham in his relationship with God. This moment will determine what God will now do through him and his descendants to fulfill His Promise of a blessing and a Savior through whom the whole earth would be blessed! This is one of the most sacred moments in all of recorded history!

The phrase, "Now it came to pass after these things" (Gen. 22:1), reminds us of God's "fullness of time." So much had to be in place before God could act decisively! Forty years of God's activity in and with Abraham had to be in place for this moment to occur. So much was in the balance. But the wonderful truth emerging here is that God's timing is always right! He knew Abraham's heart! He knew his *faith*! He knew his *obedience*! God knew that when this moment had been accomplished, He would have a sample of true *faith*, which He could account for righteousness, for the rest of time!

DAY 1

Refining Moments

This refining moment came to others throughout Biblical history. It came to Joseph in prison. Joseph's heart remained loyal to God in his darkest hour, so God could exalt him to be Pharaoh's right-hand man and bring blessing to nations, including God's chosen family. This moment came to Moses at the burning bush. Forty long years in the wilderness refined his character, so God could use him to redeem His people from Egypt. Esther was refined for years, mostly through tragedy with her people. She was steadfast in character, so God tested her (refined her further) by confronting her with pleading the case of God's people before the king. It could have cost her life! God used her to deliver His people. The list of the "heroes of the faith" found in Hebrews 11 gives but a glimpse of those approved of God through God's refining process. A study of each of them would prove very profitable, especially in helping to identify and respond to God's refining process in your own life!

Then there comes a very simple statement: "God tested Abraham" (Gen. 22:1). This may sound strange to your ears since you may remember James 1:13: "Let no one say when he is tempted, 'I am tempted by God'; for God cannot be tempted by evil, nor does He Himself tempt anyone." In this context in James, the word *tempted* is speaking of the evil nature or evil itself. Sin, not God, draws us toward our sinful nature (Gal. 5:19). Sin cannot affect God, and God never uses any form of sin to tempt anyone.

Sin cannot affect God, and God never uses any form of sin to tempt anyone.

In Genesis 22:1, God is refining and proving Abraham's true heart toward Him. God does create an opportunity for Abraham's heart to be revealed as "pure gold" with no mixture of dross (elements that are not pure gold). Forty years of God's Hand upon him have removed all that is objectionable to God, and all that would affect or hinder pure *faith* and *obedience* to anything God should ask. Abraham's immediate, thorough, and total *obedience* showed his heart toward God. Nothing less than an opportunity to obey God in His most demanding request would be sufficient for God or Abraham.

How has God refined your life? Describe how God has developed your relationship with Him.

Now there follows the simplest description of a man God could call "His friend." First, God called him by name, "Abraham!" and he answered immediately to a Voice with whom he was now familiar and a Voice he had come to trust, for he knew God loved him personally. Second, Abraham's answer was now very familiar to God, "Here I am!" He was not hiding, as Adam was when God called to him (Gen. 3:9–10).

Abraham was now "God's friend," and the fellowship with God was immediate and full.

Then comes the moment when "heaven stood still" and watched and waited as God, in love, gave a most unusual but clear and complete command:

> *Take now your son, your only son Isaac, whom you love, and go to the land of Moriah, and offer him there as a burnt offering on one of the mountains of which I shall tell you.*
>
> GENESIS 22:2

Now we see from God's Heart! God had to create a maximum moment for Abraham to express his utter *faith, love,* and *trust* in Him. *Faith* has to be expressed in a real-life situation, with clear specifics from God, in a way that demands *faith-obedience* in God! No directive from God could have been more complete for Abraham:

Faith has to be expressed in a real-life situation, with clear specifics from God, in a way that demands _faith-obedience_ in God!

1. **"Take now your son, your only son Isaac"**—all Abraham's known possibilities for a future, as far as human reasoning can understand it, were asked to be handed over. If there is to be a future, only God could reveal it. Abraham would now demonstrate complete trust in the God whom he had come to know in life for forty-plus years.

2. **"Isaac"**—not Ishmael, as he had earlier reasoned with God. Not Ishmael, his firstborn son—but not by God's promise, but his reasoning. Take the only son of promise. Take the one who for fifteen years has brought you joy.

The only possible competition to God was his greatly loved son.

3. **"Whom you love"**—the only possible competition to God was his greatly loved son. Here is where we see the many similarities to God and His only Son, whom He loved (John 3:16). Love is where the heart is, and the *faith* God was looking for must be *faith* in the heart, as pure as refined gold. Abraham

was to hold on to nothing, but release everything to God who had loved him so completely.

4. "Go to the land of Moriah . . . on one of the mountains of which I shall tell you." The best evidence we have is that the place for the sacrifice of his son was very near Calvary, where Jesus would become God's Lamb offered and sacrificed for the sin of a world. How special in God's eyes was this moment, though so much was hidden from Abraham. Abraham had gone as God had commanded when he was first called to a land known only to God and one that God would show him. The places God chooses for our sacrifice are holy to God, and become holy to us through *obedience*.

I read of a friend of mine, a missionary to the Karamojong region of East Africa. He was traveling with his wife and two children to a people God had told him to love. For four years they loved them. Now, suddenly, shots rang out and passed through their vehicle and hit a tree. All were in danger. But they were there, where God had moved them, just like Abraham. God delivered them to safety with only a few cuts and bruises. How God would do it, they did not know. That He would do it they had no doubt! Questions? Yes! As I read the account, and remember our friendship, I bow my head in real joy of my Lord and continue to pray for them and their safety. But knowing what I do about God's purposes through Abraham's *faith* and *obedience*, I also pray that many who see these missionaries' faith will put their faith in the God who delivers those He chooses, calls, and sends into our world.

List the names of people who have put their faith in God because of how they saw your faith and obedience toward Him.

- **Review what God has shown you through the lesson today.**
- **Look back over your lesson and take time to underline or highlight key statements that God used to impact your life.**
- **Write a statement here that God used most in your life today:**

- **Turn to the end of the chapter and write your statement again. This will provide a weekly list of key statements for you to meditate on the last two days of the week.**

  ❑ CHECK THIS BOX AFTER YOU HAVE DONE SO.
- **Take time to pray, asking God to adjust your life to how He has spoken to you today.**
- **With whom do you need to share this truth today?**

SUMMARY STATEMENTS

- Sin cannot affect God, and God never uses any form of sin to tempt anyone.
- Faith has to be expressed in a real-life situation, with clear specifics from God, in a way that demands faith-obedience in God!

DAY 2

ABRAHAM'S OBEDIENCE

The response of Abraham causes all heaven to break out into joy for anticipated full obedience. Obedience is a choice based on real commands from God. The process of obedience from the command to the utter fulfillment is remarkable and very real. All the emotions that can be mustered begin to surge through our minds and hearts as we identify more and more with Abraham, his son Isaac, and his servants. But our attention still must be on God through it all. The eternal purpose of God was at stake and was unfolding step by step. The entire process is full of the activity of God. God had thoroughly prepared "His friend" Abraham for this moment of *truth*, and I believe at each step God brought much to Abraham's remembrance that helped him complete his step of *faith* that became a pattern of *faith* for all of time.

Obedience is a choice based on real commands from God.

God always prepares His servants ahead of time, with much assurance, for such huge moments of faith.

First, the phrase, "So Abraham rose early in the morning," is seen not only in Genesis 22:3, but also in Genesis 21:14, when he obeyed God in sending out his "other son" Ishmael, to die also. His obedience with both Ishmael and Isaac was immediate. There was no arguing or pleading—only *faith*! God always prepares His servants ahead of time, with much assurance, for such huge moments of *faith*. Abraham had already obeyed God in sending Hagar and Ishmael away, accompanied by God's promise (Gen. 21:13). God was true to His promise then, and He would be true to His promise for Isaac.

Second, God watched as he did everything necessary for utter obedience: Abraham prepared two servants, donkeys, wood, fire, and his son, with no hesitation or delay. Too often we do not put everything in place to obey. I am recalling a recent graduation from seminary of a young man who knew God was calling him into the ministry about four years ago while attending a conference that my wife and I were leading for couples. He had inherited, as the eldest son, the family business. But God had called him. He, too, immediately informed his family and his parents, loaded up their goods, enrolled in seminary, and moved to Ft. Worth. Now, after four years of *faith* and obedience, he has graduated from seminary and is pastoring a fine church.

But others I have watched who had a similar call have postponed their obedience and are still not doing God's will. Obedience is not easy, but it does require pure *faith* in God who calls. It is in fact an Abraham kind of *faith*—immediate and thorough in its obedience. This is the only kind of *faith* that is worthy of God or acceptable to God!

Maybe this is an important moment for you to reflect and meditate and ask yourself some key questions. Has God called you?

❏ There is no doubt. ❏ I hope He has.

❏ I am not sure. ❏ I am working through that.

Has He been shaping and preparing you over the years? Are you right now at a point where you know what God has commanded next? Have you set in motion an immediate process of obedience because you trust Him? Write a testimony that would answer these questions.

____

____

____

____

____

____

There are yet other moments when Abraham's *faith* and God's pleasure are seen. Abraham speaks to his servants as they travel to the place of sacrifice and assures them, "We will come back to you" (Gen. 22:5)—what absolute assurance is seen in Abraham's heart. But it was born out of forty-plus years of failure and obedience, and experiencing more and more of God as he did. Now it all came together in this special moment before God.

Also, his *faith* is expressed in greater depth when his son Isaac, whom he loves, suddenly asks a heart-penetrating question, "My father! . . . Look, the fire and the wood, but where is the lamb for a burnt offering?" (Gen. 22:7). Heaven again awaits his reply, "My son, God will provide for Himself the lamb for a burnt offering" (Gen. 22:8). What went through Abraham's heart at this moment?

What went through your mind the last time God asked you to obey Him?

____

____

____

Hebrews 11:17–19 gives us a window into his soul:

> *By faith Abraham, when he was tested, offered up Isaac, and he who had received the promises offered up his only begotten son, of whom it was said, "In Isaac your seed shall be called," concluding that God was able to raise him up, even from the dead, from which he also received him in a figurative sense.*

Only the most intimate of a love-relationship could answer with such clarity and assurance! We know God was watching and listening to every word and reading his heart, for when Abraham released his son completely to God, God responded by saying,

> *Now I know that you fear God, since you have not withheld your son, your only son, from Me.*
>
> GENESIS 22:12

The final moment of expressed love and *faith* was the sacrifice itself. Abraham placed the wood in order, bound his son, laid him on the altar, and took the knife to slay his son! Each step carried with it more *faith*! No record is given of his conversation, if any, with his son Isaac. But it is obvious that Isaac, too, was trusting God—the God of his father's utter *faith*, which Abraham had instilled in him from the time he could understand. In many ways, it was here, at this moment, that Isaac appropriated Abraham's *faith*. They were obeying God together! They knew it, but more so God knew it. Abraham had begun his walk with God—or rather, God began His walk with Abraham by a huge step of *faith* and obedience. Now God begins His continued Covenant with Isaac, in an exceptional step of *faith* by both Abraham and his son.

Once again there is a Divine intervention, but now it comes after a step of *faith*! Again and again, throughout his life, God carefully and lovingly intervened in Abraham's life. In each intervention Abraham experienced new understanding of God and of His Covenant. Because of this he also responded with a new dimension of *faith*. He had lived "from faith to faith": "For in it the righteousness of God is revealed from faith to faith; as it is written, 'The just shall live by faith'" (Rom. 1:17).

The book of Hebrews adds a very important element to this truth, and does so immediately before God's definition of *faith* and the record of the heroes of *faith*:

> *Now the just shall live by faith;*
> *But if anyone draws back,*
> *My soul has no pleasure in him.*
>
> HEBREWS 10:38

How simple and direct is the record! "But the Angel of the LORD called to him from heaven and said, 'Abraham, Abraham!' So he said, 'Here I am'" (Gen. 22:11). This time his name was called twice, giving urgency to God's call! By now the Voice of God came to Abraham as a Friend!

Here, no mention is ever given of the tone of God's Voice. But to Abraham, God's Voice brought immediate obedience. God Himself did not stay his hand! His Voice caused Abraham to cease his sacrifice of his son. But again, the Scriptures themselves indicate that the sacrifice had thoroughly and irrevocably been made in his heart, "concluding that God was able to raise him up, even from the dead" (Heb. 11:19).

Abraham's friendship with God was greater than his intense love for his only son, Isaac.

Abraham's friendship with God was greater than his intense love for his only son, Isaac. It had to be this way with God! There could be no competition in Abraham's heart, not even his dearest and most prized possession, his son! Pure love for and trust in God were the only *faith* worthy of God and therefore the only *faith* acceptable to God! For this *faith* God would grant righteousness in exchange (Gen. 15:6; Rom. 4:3, 9, 22). The relationship was completed with God in this act of ultimate sacrifice in obedience! This step of *faith* was to God and Him alone. It should be noted that as *faith* that saves is to God alone, so sin is against God and Him only (Ps. 51:4). David, when he sinned, said,

> *Against You, You only, have I sinned,*
> *And done this evil in Your sight—*
> *That You may be found just when You speak,*

And blameless when You judge.
Behold, I was brought forth in iniquity,
And in sin my mother conceived me.

PSALM 51:4–5

- **Review what God has shown you through the lesson today.**
- **Look back over your lesson and take time to underline or highlight key statements that God used to impact your life.**
- **Write a statement here that God used most in your life today:**

____

____

____

- **Turn to the end of the chapter and write your statement again. This will provide a weekly list of key statements for you to meditate on the last two days of the week.**

  ❑ CHECK THIS BOX AFTER YOU HAVE DONE SO.
- **Take time to pray, asking God to adjust your life to how He has spoken to you today.**
- **With whom do you need to share this truth today?**

____

SUMMARY STATEMENTS

- Obedience is a choice based on real commands from God.
- God always prepares His servants ahead of time, with much assurance, for such huge moments of faith.
- Your friendship with God must be greater than your love for anyone else.

DAY 3

PERSONAL OBEDIENCE

On a much lesser scale, my wife and I went through this experience with God, and we have never been the same since. We have come to know Him so deeply, and have more trust in Him today than ever before—and more blessings from Him in our lives and our "descendants" (our children). God graciously gave us four boys and one girl. From the very beginning, even as we held our firstborn son, we knew God had a wonderful plan for each of them. As all parents we thought one might be a lawyer (to take care of any legal needs we might have); one surely would be a doctor (to take care of any physical needs we might have); one would in his profession make lots of money (to take care of our financial needs in old age); maybe one would be a pastor (to help us in our spiritual needs); and one might be a missionary (to fulfill our commitment to missions). In all our dreams for our children we always added, "But not our will, but Yours be done, O Lord!" We meant this with all our hearts.

We then sought carefully to raise our children to love and trust and obey our Lord! We faithfully modeled for them the joy of serving God with all our hearts. Then one day in a worship service where I was preaching, our oldest son, a university student with much promise to be a lawyer, came forward with tears, declaring that God was "calling him into the ministry." He said he had been running from God's call, but could do so no longer. With tears we all rejoiced and felt honored God had called one of ours. It was not long after, when our second son came forward in another service where I was preaching, indicating clearly that God was calling him, too, into some form of full-time ministry. Again we rejoiced and felt overwhelmed that God would claim two of our sons.

Several years later I was speaking in another city to a student conference. Afterward I noticed two of my children talking while standing outside the pastor's study. They said to me, "Dad, we are praying for our third brother," who, they said, "was experiencing God in the same way we did—you know, Dad, when God called us!"

We rejoiced there in prayer! Sure enough, when our third son emerged, with eyes red from weeping, he announced that he had surrendered his life to his Lord for the ministry! Once again, we rejoiced, releasing another son afresh to our Lord, and asked God to help us raise our three sons to honor and serve Him.

A few years later, I was sharing a message to college students at a conference center in Glorieta, New Mexico. Many hundreds of students were there, including our entire family. Someone came running to me after the service, saying, "Do you know that your teenage daughter went forward at the altar call giving her life to God to be a missionary?" I rejoiced again, and sought her out to assure her that the highest honor God could ever bestow on us as a family was for Him to choose and call one of ours to Himself. We all rejoiced!

Our fourth son in college was struggling with his relationship with God. He did not want to be just like his brothers, so he set his heart to study criminal justice. He did well. But following a service in a church where I was preaching, he asked to talk with me. He had not walked as faithfully with God as our other children, but never got away from his sensitive heart toward God. We went to a restaurant after the service, and he said, "Dad, I'm sorry for all the hurt I may have caused you and Mom. But, Dad, I want you to know God is calling me into the ministry!"

I stood in a crowded restaurant and hugged my son unashamedly and with tears I said, "O God! You are a faithful God, just like You promised!"

We yielded all five of our precious children to our Lord and made a covenant to pray for every step they would take from their point of call.

Today, each of them has married a godly marriage partner and is serving the Lord faithfully.

- Our oldest completed a Ph.D. and is a wonderful seminary president in Canada, having first pastored a church for five years (part of that time having his brother next to him serving with him as an associate pastor).
- Our second son has served two years in Norway and several churches as youth or music minister and is now associate pastor in a church in Canada, sensing God is ready to have him serve some church as the senior pastor. He is enrolled to complete further training in a D.Min. degree.
- Our third son is pastoring a church in Canada, having finished a Ph.D. from the seminary.
- Our fourth son is pastoring a church in Texas while he completes his Ph.D.
- Our daughter has finished her seminary training and is waiting on her husband to complete his seminary training. They are planning to serve God as career missionaries.

So, we do not have in our family a lawyer, or a doctor, or a son making lots of money! But we have four pastors and a missionary plus their marriage partners and ten grandchildren—and God, who will take good care of us. The command had come to us, one child at a time, to release them to be wholly His. We heard Him call our names for the sacrifice and we obeyed. And as He did with Abraham, He gave our children back to us fully ready to serve Him (none of them live close to us, but we have phones and E-mail!).

What sacrifice has God asked of you, and how have you obeyed?

____

____

ABRAHAM'S AWE OF GOD

Now God's Voice of Divine intervention again commanded, "Abraham, Abraham!" And Abraham again replied simply, "Here I am!" And God, with all of heaven rejoicing, said, "Do not lay your hand on the lad, or do anything to him; for now I know that you fear God, since you have not withheld your son, your only son, from Me" (Gen. 22:12).

After more than forty years of shaping Abraham to be "His friend," the process was complete! Several truths must be noticed, for they will be present in your walk with God as you go farther with Him.

First, it was in an act of obedience to a specific command of God that God knew Abraham's heart was fixed to love and trust Him. It is never what we say to God but what we do toward God once He has spoken to us!

An act of obedience is never what we say to God but what we do toward God once He has spoken to us!

Jesus confirmed this in many ways as He sought to bring His disciples to this same kind of *faith.* Jesus said, "Not everyone who says to Me, 'Lord, Lord,' shall enter the kingdom of heaven, but he who does the will of My Father in heaven" (Matt. 7:21).

To enter the kingdom of heaven does not mean to go to heaven when you die. It will include this. But it means to enter into the fullest experience of God's rule and reign in one's life and world. It means, like Abraham, to experience God and His Presence with you in ever-increasing measure, in the here and now and in the hereafter!

Second, what God was looking for was one who feared God. God said, "Now I know that you fear [Me]" (Gen. 22:12). This may surprise many. We may have thought that He would have said, "Now I know that you love Me or trust Me!" However, the experience in the Bible, especially the Old Testament (but also the New Testament—e.g., Acts 2:43; 5:5, 11; 9:31; 19:17), is that God wants us first to "fear Him."

Take time to read each of these Scriptures: Acts 2:43; 5:5, 11; 9:31; 19:17. Make notes of key thoughts in the space provided here.

Moses became fearfully aware of this later and said to God's people:

> *And now, Israel, what does the* LORD *your God require of you, but to fear the* LORD *your God, to walk in all His ways and to love Him, to serve the* LORD *your God with all your heart and with all your soul, and to keep the commandments of the* LORD *and His statutes which I command you today for your good?*
>
> DEUTERONOMY 10:12–13

And he added,

> *You shall fear the* LORD *your God; you shall serve Him, and to Him you shall hold fast, and take oaths in His name. He is your praise, and He is your God, who has done for you these great and awesome things which your eyes have seen.*
>
> DEUTERONOMY 10:20–21

To God, when one "fears" Him, it is because he knows Him by firsthand experience and in that experience has come to know His love. God knows that when one fears and loves Him, he will trust Him, serve Him, keep His commands, and hold fast to Him with all his heart and soul. This Abraham did, and God acknowledged that Abraham truly did fear Him. God knows that "the fear of God is the beginning of all wisdom" (Ps. 111:10; Job 28:28; Prov. 1:7; 9:10). Even Solomon wrote at the conclusion of Ecclesiastes,

> *Let us hear the conclusion of the whole matter:*
> *Fear God and keep His commandments,*
> *For this is man's all.*
>
> ECCLESIASTES 12:13

The Amplified Bible puts it even more profoundly,

> *All has been heard. The end of the matter is, Fear God—know that He is, revere and worship Him—and keep His commandments; for this is the whole of man [the full original purpose of His creation, the object of God's providence, the root of character, the foundation of all happiness, the adjustment to all inharmonious circumstances and conditions under the sun, and the whole duty for every man].*
>
> ECCLESIASTES 12:13

This is an accurate picture of Abraham in his relationship with God. He had learned who his God was, and he trembled, in awe of Him. His fear of God led him to take this ultimate step of *faith* and *obedience* to God. God knew that his response was with his whole heart and soul.

His fear of God led him to take this ultimate step of *faith* and *obedience* to God.

- **Review what God has shown you through the lesson today.**
- **Look back over your lesson and take time to underline or highlight key statements that God used to impact your life.**
- **Write a statement here that God used most in your life today:**

___

___

___

- **Turn to the end of the chapter and write your statement again. This will provide a weekly list of key statements for you to meditate on the last two days of the week.**

  ❑ CHECK THIS BOX AFTER YOU HAVE DONE SO.
- **Take time to pray, asking God to adjust your life to how He has spoken to you today.**
- **With whom do you need to share this truth today?**

___

SUMMARY STATEMENTS

- An act of obedience is never what we say to God but what we do toward God once He has spoken to us!
- The fear of God leads us to take an ultimate step of faith and obedience to God.

DAY 4

THE PATTERN OF FAITH

God intervened, and Abraham knew that God was "Provider"! Abraham saw a ram caught in the bushes and took God's provision of a substitute for his son, and completed the sacrifice and worship to God. He had told his son earlier, "My son, God will provide for Himself the lamb for a burnt offering" (Gen. 22:8). God

Himself had indeed provided a ram—for Himself—for Abraham to use in his *obedience*. The provision for our obedience is always provided for us by God. Ours is to obey; it is for God to provide! What we in our weakness and limitations cannot provide, God in His infinite grace does provide.

The provision for our obedience is always provided for us by God. Ours is to obey; it is for God to provide!

Peter experienced this when he had fished all night and caught nothing. Jesus asked him to fish one more time. This time he would do what Jesus asked, and God provided the fish. Peter believed God when God provided (Luke 5:1–11). Obedience brings God's provision. Abraham named the place where God provided after God—Jehovah-Jireh, "the Lord will provide"! Abraham never ceased to tell others of the mighty works of God, and for centuries it was said among God's people, to encourage them, "And Abraham called the name of the place, The-LORD-Will-Provide; as it is said to this day, 'In the Mount of the LORD it shall be provided'" (Gen. 22:14).

Words utterly fail us to describe the ultimate fulfillment of this saying on a nearby mount called Calvary. It was there also that God provided. Because of our sin, each of us was to die ("the wages of sin is death" [Rom. 6:23]). But God intervened for us with a Substitute—His Own Son. This time the deathblow fell, and His Own Son died as a sacrifice to God for our sin. The writer of Hebrews said, "Christ was offered once to bear the sins of many . . . For by one offering He has perfected forever those who are being sanctified" (Heb. 9:28; 10:14). Paul described so carefully how God provided salvation for all who would believe, through the death of His Son, saying,

> *But now the righteousness of God apart from the law is revealed, being witnessed by the Law and the Prophets, even the righteousness of God, through faith in Jesus Christ, to all and on all who believe. For there is no difference; for all have sinned and fall short of the glory of God, being justified freely by His grace through the redemption that is in Christ Jesus, whom God set forth as a propitiation by His blood, through faith, to demonstrate His righteousness, because in His forbearance God had passed over the sins that were previously committed, to demonstrate at the present time His righteousness, that He might be just and the justifier of the one who has faith in Jesus.*
>
> ROMANS 3:21–26

John was right when he pointed to Jesus and said, "Behold! The Lamb of God who takes away the sin of the world!" (John 1:29).

The scene on Mount Moriah with Abraham and Isaac, and God's intervening with a ram as a substitute, was repeated on Calvary. But this time God did not stay His Hand, but "made Him who knew no sin to be sin for us, that we might become the righteousness of God in Him" (2 Cor. 5:21). The sacrifice of God's Son was made, and it was acceptable to God for our sin.

> *Yet it pleased the* LORD *to bruise Him;*
> *He has put Him to grief.*
> *When You make His soul an offering for sin,*
> *He shall see His seed, He shall prolong His days,*
> *And the pleasure of the* LORD *shall prosper in His hand.*
> *He shall see the labor of His soul, and be satisfied.*
> *By His knowledge My righteous Servant shall justify many,*
> *For He shall bear their iniquities.*

ISAIAH 53:10–11

Now all who believe Him and what He has provided for them, repent of their sin, and place their faith in Him, He gives them eternal life (John 3:16).

Now we understand what God was doing. Abraham believed God, and God attributed that *faith-obedience* to him for righteousness. Everyone to the end of time who puts his trust in God as Abraham did would be saved from his sin. Have you believed Him and received from God what He has provided for you, in the life, death, and resurrection of His Son? If not, would you do that now, by *faith*, in prayer?

GOD'S PROMISES

But God was not finished. He had so much more to share with Abraham, and He began in Genesis 22:15–18:

> *Then the Angel of the* LORD *called to Abraham a second time out of heaven, and said: "By Myself I have sworn, says the* LORD*, because you have done this thing, and have not withheld your son, your only son—blessing I will bless you, and multiplying I will multiply your descendants as the stars of the heaven and as the sand which is on the seashore; and your descendants shall possess the gate of their enemies. In your seed all the nations of the earth shall be blessed, because you have obeyed My voice."*

God brought full circle His earlier promises and spoke them in one final promise to Abraham. Look carefully at the truths expressed in this relationship with Abraham, "His friend":

GOD'S PROMISES TO ABRAHAM

1. God took the initiative to establish a sure Covenant: "By Myself I have sworn."

2. Abraham's obedience was the key to God in His Covenant: It was so in the first Covenant, and it was so here: "Because you have done this thing . . . because you have obeyed My voice" (vv. 16, 18).

3. God would bless Him: "Blessing I will bless you."

4. He would multiply his seed: "Multiplying I will multiply your descendants."

5. God would deal with any who would come against him or his descendants: "Your descendants shall possess the gate of their enemies."

6. God would bless all the nations of the earth through his seed: "In your seed all the nations of the earth shall be blessed." From now to the end of time both Abraham and his descendants would be instruments through which He would bring blessing to all the nations of the world! Preeminently, it would come through a direct descendant—Jesus (Matt. 1:1–2; Luke 3:34).

God had an eternal plan, to bring His great salvation to every nation and every people group. He chose to begin with Abraham and his descendants. Through them He would build a nation for Himself. They would be to Him a "holy nation . . . and a kingdom of priests" (Ex. 19:3–6; 1 Peter 2:9–10). Through this special people He would bring the Messiah, His Own Son. Through His Son He would bring His salvation and make it available to all people, in all ages. Abraham was therefore very special to God. And through him all who come after him were special. But not merely his physical descendants, but his spiritual descendants, those who have and express the *faith* of Abraham (Rom. 4:1–12). It climaxes with Paul assuring the Gentiles "that he might be the father of all those who believe, though they are uncircumcised, that righteousness might be imputed to them also, and the father of circumcision to those who not only are of the circumcision, but who also walk in the steps of the faith which our father Abraham had while still uncircumcised" (Rom. 4:11–12).

So Paul continued to stress that the "heirs" of Abraham include also those Gentiles who have the *faith* of Abraham:

> *Therefore it is of faith that it might be according to grace, so that the promise might be sure to all the seed, not only to those who are of the law, but also to those who are of the faith of Abraham, who is the father of us all (as it is written, "I have made you a father of many nations") in the presence of Him whom he believed—God, who gives life to the dead and calls those things which do not exist as though they did; who, contrary to hope, in hope believed, so that he became the father of many nations, according to what was spoken, "So shall your descendants be." And not being weak in faith, he did not consider his own body, already dead (since he was about a hundred years old), and the deadness of*

Sarah's womb. He did not waver at the promise of God through unbelief, but was strengthened in faith, giving glory to God, and being fully convinced that what He had promised He was also able to perform. And therefore "it was accounted to him for righteousness." Now it was not written for his sake alone that it was imputed to him, but also for us. It shall be imputed to us who believe in Him who raised up Jesus our Lord from the dead, who was delivered up because of our offenses, and was raised because of our justification.

ROMANS 4:16–25

Read this passage very carefully and see how Abraham's *faith* became the pattern of *faith* for all mankind, the *faith* that saves, or the *faith* that God "accounts for righteousness" (vv. 22–25).

Paul clearly connected the *faith* of Abraham, now firmly established and affirmed by God, to the Gentiles of his day and therefore to us today in this passage: "For you are all sons of God through faith in Christ Jesus. For as many of you as were baptized into Christ have put on Christ. There is neither Jew nor Greek, there is neither slave nor free, there is neither male nor female; for you are all one in Christ Jesus" (Gal. 3:26–28). Hear it again: "And if you are Christ's, then you are Abraham's seed, and heirs according to the promise" (Gal. 3:29).

Are you sensing the excitement of your relationship with God—by faith? Describe the excitement.

____

____

____

____

____

How would you compare your faith in Christ as the work of God in you, even as it was in Abraham?

____

____

____

Revisit some of the life-affecting moments that you have encountered. Ask God to help you see them from His perspective. How has He made

you aware of His Presence and His activity and His purposes in those times?

____

____

____

There is another truth here that you may need to visit! The bottom line with God, always, is seen in His final word with Abraham: "Because you have obeyed My voice" (Gen. 22:18). Every time God approves and blesses Abraham He says it is because he heard His Voice and knew that it was God who was speaking to him; he knew what God was saying to him; he knew what he was to do next, once God had spoken to him; and he obeyed God and obeyed immediately, thoroughly, and with great *faith* in God! This is what God is looking for! This is what God is always looking for! This is still what God is looking for! It can best be expressed in the words of the prophet Hanani when he spoke for God to King Asa: "For the eyes of the LORD run to and fro throughout the whole earth, to show Himself strong on behalf of those whose heart is loyal to Him" (2 Chron. 16:9).

The key to an effective and powerful walk with God is always obedience. Jesus expressed this vital element in those who would walk with Him when He said to the crowd, "Why do you call Me 'Lord, Lord,' and not do the things which I say?" (Luke 6:46). Jesus then went on to deepen the significance of obedience in all of life by using a parable to picture clearly the effect of obedience, especially to God:

The key to an effective and powerful walk with God is always obedience.

> *Whoever comes to Me, and hears My sayings and does them, I will show you whom he is like: He is like a man building a house, who dug deep and laid the foundation on the rock. And when the flood arose, the stream beat vehemently against that house, and could not shake it, for it was founded on the rock. But he who heard and did nothing is like a man who built a house on the earth without a foundation, against which the stream beat vehemently; and immediately it fell. And the ruin of that house was great.*
>
> LUKE 6:47–49

Obedience is our very life, with God!

Notice how utterly devastating is the person who comes to Him; hears what He says; and does not do it! Obedience to God is not a minor matter. Obedience is our very life, with God! It should again be remembered that "partial obedience" is really disobedience with God! This is true for every person.

It should again be remembered that "partial obedience" is really disobedience with God!

God plays no favorites and makes no exceptions! The writer James made this truth devastatingly clear when in his letter to believers he said, "For whoever shall keep the whole law, and yet stumble in one point, he is guilty of all" (James 2:10).

God would say, "Faith, without obedience by works, is dead!" Let's revisit an essential further discussion by James where he used Abraham precisely in his offering of Isaac to help the readers understand, from God's perspective, what kind of *faith* it is that is acceptable to God and saves a person: "Faith by itself, if it does not have works, is dead . . . You see then that a man is justified by works, and not by faith only" (James 2:17, 24).

Today, too many are convinced that all God is looking for in their belief in Him is a verbal statement of *faith*! This is not true and never has been true. God said to Abraham that now He knew he believed Him, and feared Him, because he "obeyed My voice" and did what God commanded, offered up his only son, the son he loved.

Now—read this verse again, for this is the heart of the entire book:

> *And the Scripture was fulfilled which says, "Abraham believed God, and it was accounted to him for righteousness." And he was called the friend of God.*
>
> JAMES 2:23

- **Review what God has shown you through the lesson today.**
- **Look back over your lesson and take time to underline or highlight key statements that God used to impact your life.**
- **Write a statement here that God used most in your life today:**

____

____

____

- **Turn to the end of the chapter and write your statement again. This will provide a weekly list of key statements for you to meditate on the last two days of the week.**

  ❑ CHECK THIS BOX AFTER YOU HAVE DONE SO.
- **Take time to pray, asking God to adjust your life to how He has spoken to you today.**
- **With whom do you need to share this truth today?**

____

Summary Statements

- The provision for our obedience is always provided for us by God. Ours is to obey; it is for God to provide!
- The key to an effective and powerful walk with God is always obedience.
- Obedience to God is not a minor matter. Obedience is our very life, with God!
- It should again be remembered that "partial obedience" is really disobedience with God!

DAY 5

The Process

I return to the process God used with Abraham that led him to be called a "friend of God." It is so important to see it clearly and believe it is truly God's way for us, too.

First, Abraham knew the Voice of God and therefore knew when God was speaking.

Do you clearly, unmistakably know the Voice of God when He is speaking to you?

❑ I am certain. ❑ I'm not sure anyone can know.

❑ I am not sure. ❑ It is obvious to me most of the time.

If not, you are in trouble at the heart of your relationship with God. I am not talking about hearing an audible voice but rather learning to hear the Voice of God through the Scriptures. How can you obey Him if you never know when He is speaking? If obedience to His Voice was the key to Abraham's relationship with God, as we have seen in Genesis 22:18, then obedience to God's Voice is crucial to our relationship with God![1]

I am not talking about hearing an audible voice but rather learning to hear the Voice of God through the Scriptures.

I have pastored for almost thirty years and worked with God's people for forty-three years. The cry I hear most often from God's people has been, "How can God—Father, Son, and Holy Spirit—be more real and personal to me, and how can I clearly know and do the will of God?"

I have spent a lifetime helping God's people with these two questions. In the simplest of answers I would say:

1. *Be convinced that God really does speak to His people.* This is revealed from Genesis (where He is speaking to Adam and Eve) to Revelation (where He is speaking to John), and throughout every book in the Bible.

2. *Realize thoroughly that those He spoke to always knew it was God*, always knew what He was saying, and always knew what they were to do.

3. *Believe, from Scripture, that therefore God speaks to you, too.* However, a warning is needed here. Do not bring the Scriptures down to the level of your experience (i.e., by saying, "He has never spoken to me; therefore I am convinced He does not speak to His people anymore"). Ask God to help you bring your experience up to the level of the Word of God.

4. *Determine to learn, from Scripture, how He speaks.* But first believe that He speaks. In Scripture He speaks to each person uniquely. But each person always knows it is God. Believe Jesus when He urged His disciples, in the Sermon on the Mount,

> *Ask, and it will be given to you; seek, and you will find; knock, and it will be opened to you. For everyone who asks receives, and he who seeks finds, and to him who knocks it will be opened. Or what man is there among you who, if his son asks for bread, will give him a stone? Or if he asks for a fish, will he give him a serpent? If you then, being evil, know how to give good gifts to your children, how much more will your Father who is in heaven give good things to those who ask Him!*
>
> MATTHEW 7:7–11

You can be a "friend of God"! It is a choice of the heart!

Notice and believe that Jesus said, "Everyone." Believe that in the word *everyone* you are included, and act on it. Ask! Seek! Knock! And you will receive. But when you do, obey immediately, thoroughly, and with great *faith* as Abraham did! God will confirm to you His Presence and His favor and blessing. You can be a "friend of God"! It is a choice of the heart! God, who invited Abraham to "walk before Me and be blameless" (Gen. 17:1), invites you to do the same! Jesus invited Peter to "follow Me and I will make you become . . ." (Matt. 4:19; Mark 1:17). And the Apostle Paul urged,

> *I, therefore, the prisoner of the Lord, beseech you to walk worthy of the calling with which you were called, with all lowliness and gentleness, with longsuffering, bearing with one another in love, endeavoring to keep the unity of the Spirit in the bond of peace.*
>
> EPHESIANS 4:1–3

Now His invitation comes to you. The Holy Spirit is your Guide and Teacher. Jesus said,

> *But the Helper, the Holy Spirit, whom the Father will send in My name, He will teach you all things, and bring to your remembrance all things that I said to you.*
>
> JOHN 14:26

> *However, when He, the Spirit of truth, has come, He will guide you into all truth; for He will not speak on His own authority, but whatever He hears He will speak; and He will tell you things to come. He will glorify Me, for He will take of what is Mine and declare it to you. All things that the Father has are Mine. Therefore I said that He will take of Mine and declare it to you.*
>
> JOHN 16:13–15

This is for you!

In my own life, as I have studied the Scriptures (such as the life of Abraham) I have believed I was always face-to-Face with God. His Spirit is always present, doing what the Father assigned for Him to do with me—teach me, guide me, and enable me—in my personal walk with God. So I knew He alone could reveal God's purposes and ways to me, and when He did, I knew that I must obey and do it from a deep and personal relationship of love with Him. As I have done this over many years I have never known God to fail me or leave me, but always to enable me just as He did Abraham. I have always believed that I could be a "friend of God" by God's Own choice, just as He chose Abraham. This is why a very close study of God's initiatives with Abraham is so important. Genesis does not show me how Abraham walked with God—though I can see it that way if I choose. Rather, Genesis reveals to me how God fulfilled His eternal purpose through a man called Abraham. This is how I choose to read the Scripture, so when God is working in my life, I will know it is God, know what I need to do, and obey Him—immediately, thoroughly, and with *great faith.*

GOD'S PURPOSES INCLUDED ABRAHAM'S DESCENDANTS

So much of God's Covenant with Abraham surfaces in his son Isaac, and his son Jacob, and his son Joseph. God's relationship with Abraham is used throughout the rest of Biblical history, to help each succeeding generation to:

1. Know the nature of His Covenant with those He chooses.
2. Know how to recognize His Voice to them.

3. Be convinced of how very serious such a call of God is on those He chooses.
4. Help them to obey Him, for His eternal purposes.
5. Know how severe His dealings are with those He chooses who refuse to obey Him.
6. Constantly realize the eternal consequences for those who choose to be "on mission with Him" to bless "all the nations of the earth" through them.
7. Enable them to respond to Him, as Abraham did.

It is immediately obvious that Abraham was careful to instruct Isaac by sharing all he knew from his own experience with God. This obviously included how to recognize God's Voice and respond to Him. It also included the importance of building an altar and calling on God's Name: "And the LORD appeared to him the same night and said, 'I am the God of your father Abraham; do not fear, for I am with you. I will bless you and multiply your descendants for My servant Abraham's sake.' So he built an altar there and called on the name of the LORD, and he pitched his tent there; and there Isaac's servants dug a well" (Gen. 26:24–25).

Isaac in turn told all to his son Jacob! Jacob also, on meeting God, set up a stone for a special place to remember his meeting with God:

> *Then Jacob awoke from his sleep and said, "Surely the* LORD *is in this place, and I did not know it." And he was afraid and said, "How awesome is this place! This is none other than the house of God, and this is the gate of heaven!" Then Jacob rose early in the morning, and took the stone that he had put at his head, set it up as a pillar, and poured oil on top of it. And he called the name of that place Bethel; but the name of that city had been Luz previously. Then Jacob made a vow, saying, "If God will be with me, and keep me in this way that I am going, and give me bread to eat and clothing to put on, so that I come back to my father's house in peace, then the* LORD *shall be my God. And this stone which I have set as a pillar shall be God's house, and of all that You give me I will surely give a tenth to You."*
>
> **GENESIS 28:16–22**

That same moment in Jacob's life became a reminder God used to affirm him at a crucial moment later in his life: "I am the God of Bethel, where you anointed the pillar and where you made a vow to Me. Now arise, get out of this land, and return to the land of your family" (Gen. 31:13). But again, it is so important to see God's closeness to Abraham's descendants from God's perspective. That is how we must see God's relationship with us (not merely our relationship with Him).

In the truest sense, Abraham could not pass on his *faith* to Isaac, his son, or to his grandsons. He could faithfully live out before them his *faith* in God. He could share consistently and diligently all he knew of God and all he had experienced with God. He could tell of all the mighty deeds of God. And he could urge them to carefully worship God, know and love God, and immediately obey God. He could strongly impress on them the consequences of not walking in all the ways of God. He could sensitively tell them of all the incredible blessings of *faith-obedience* with God. But he could not transfer his *faith* to them. Isaac and each of his sons would have to choose the walk of *faith* with their God! There was no automatic transfer of *faith* from father to son. It was a choice to be made by each generation for itself.

There was no automatic transfer of *faith* from father to son. It was a choice to be made by each generation for itself.

But it must be noted, from God's perspective, that He would work constantly in Isaac, as He did with Abraham, his father. As a matter of fact, when God's initiatives with Isaac are closely examined, there are many clear similarities to Abraham. Was this because Abraham had indeed shared faithfully with Isaac so if he should encounter something similar in his life, he could know it was God and know what to do? This knowledge ahead of time would create a maximum opportunity to make right choices in Isaac's life. Here are some similarities, from God's perspective:

- First, like Sarah, Rebekah, Isaac's wife, was barren (had no children). So Isaac "pleaded with the LORD for his wife" (Gen. 25:21), and God heard his cry and granted him a child.
- Second, like Abraham, he had two sons and the firstborn would not carry the Covenant blessing. Neither Ishmael (Abraham's firstborn) nor Esau (Isaac's firstborn) was to be chosen by God to inherit the Covenant blessing (Gen. 25:23). Isaac would inherit the blessing from Abraham, and Jacob would inherit the blessing from Isaac. It is important to know, from God, which of your children are chosen by God. Though we always love our firstborn, that child has to be chosen of God.
- Third, there came a famine in the land, and Isaac faced a similar choice as his father, Abraham—turn to the world for help, or seek help and counsel from the Lord (Gen. 26:1). But this time God intervened and warned Isaac: "Then the LORD appeared to him and said: 'Do not go down to Egypt; live in the land of which I shall tell you. Dwell in this land, and I will be with you and bless you; for to you and your descendants I give all these lands, and I will perform the oath which I

swore to Abraham your father'" (Gen. 26:2–3). Again, God told Isaac that his obedience would be crucial, even as it was with his father, Abraham.

- Fourth, Isaac obeyed immediately!
- Fifth, he made the same mistake as his father, Abraham, by deceiving the king of the Philistines concerning his wife, Rebekah. Isaac was graciously protected, and his life and family were spared, too.
- Sixth, his herdsmen quarreled with the Philistine herdsmen again over water. Isaac acted in peace, as his father, Abraham, did (Gen. 26:17–23).
- Seventh, God "appeared to him the same night and said, 'I am the God of your father Abraham; do not fear, for I am with you. I will bless you and multiply your descendants for My servant Abraham's sake'" (Gen. 26:24).
- Eighth, Isaac "built an altar there and called on the name of the LORD" (Gen. 26:25), just as his father did. After each encounter with God, Isaac and his family worshiped. His family watched the *faith* and *obedience* of their father, Isaac. No doubt he used each worship time as an occasion to remind his children of the God they served.
- Ninth, it may seem simple and ordinary, but from God's perspective Jacob was separated from the influence of Esau, as Isaac was from Ishmael. God had to teach each one He chose how to walk uniquely with Him, without negative family influence and conflict.

We need not pursue the descendants farther than Jacob and Joseph. But both had very significant encounters with God where each was assured by God's Presence, Protection, and Blessing. The record is in Genesis 28–50.

A summary of the process of God's shaping the one He chooses into a man of *faith* and one He can call "His friend" may be helpful again now:

I. WHAT YOU MUST DO:

A. You must hear God's Voice.

B. You must obey Him immediately, thoroughly, and with great *faith*.

C. With every encounter with God you must "build an altar" and worship—with your family and friends.

D. You must learn to wait on God to direct your steps, especially when unexpected crisis comes upon you.

E. You must accept correction from God and return to your relationship of trust when you fail.

F. Anticipate that God will reveal more of Himself to you the more you trust Him. If you are faithful in a little, He will give you more (Luke 8:18). Be ready to step out in *faith* from the greater revelation of Himself.

II. WHAT YOU CAN EXPECT GOD TO DO:

A. He will regularly affirm His Covenant relationship with you.

B. He will regularly reveal His Covenant by intervening in your life and saving you out of your failures.

C. He will affirm His Covenant with you by openly blessing you with victory and blessings so all will know He is your God, and you are His servant.

D. He will constantly reveal more and more of Himself so you can grow in your *faith*. The more you know of God, the more you can trust Him and obey Him. This is an open-ended Covenant of love!

- **Review what God has shown you through the lesson today.**
- **Look back over your lesson and take time to underline or highlight key statements that God used to impact your life.**
- **Write a statement here that God used most in your life today:**

____

____

____

- **Turn to the end of the chapter and write your statement again. This will provide a weekly list of key statements for you to meditate on the last two days of the week.**

  ❏ CHECK THIS BOX AFTER YOU HAVE DONE SO.
- **Take time to pray, asking God to adjust your life to how He has spoken to you today.**
- **With whom do you need to share this truth today?**

____

SUMMARY STATEMENTS

- I am not talking about hearing an audible voice but rather learning to hear the Voice of God through the Scriptures.
- You can be a "friend of God"! It is a choice of the heart!
- There was no automatic transfer of faith from father to son. It was a choice to be made by each generation for itself.

KEY STATEMENTS FOR MEDITATION

Day 1

Day 2

Day 3

Day 4

Day 5

UNIT 12

ABRAHAM—CONCLUDING CHAPTER

Thought Starter

Let us hear the conclusion of the whole matter:
Fear God and keep His commandments,
For this is man's all.
For God will bring every work into judgment,
Including every secret thing,
Whether good or evil.

Ecclesiastes 12:13–14

We have begun with God in His eternal counsels. We have sought a bigger picture of the purposes of God, so we could more clearly seek to understand God's place for Abraham. We noticed the initiative of God in coming to Abraham. He saw a man who worshiped Him with a pure heart. God knew that if He called Abraham to follow Him, he would respond immediately, thoroughly, and with *faith* and *obedience*!

Knowing that only God could shape a person He could use, we have followed God's activity in Abraham's life. We have noticed that His servant Abraham would not always make the right choices, seeking God's counsel first. Waiting on God first would take time and experience with God. But God made a Covenant with Abraham. God would at all times, under all circumstances, keep His Covenant. God would save his life and bring him in ever-increasing measure to know Him and trust Him completely.

In each major circumstance, Abraham would be brought through to victory. In real-life circumstances God would reveal more and more of Himself to Abraham. Each time he knew more of God by experiencing new dimensions of His nature in real life, Abraham could and would trust God further. He grew in *faith* in the measure that he came to know God. And through each real-life experience with God, in which he believed God, he grew in his character to be more like the God he served.

DAY 1

God's Initial Encounter—in Ur

It is one thing to know and have God as "our Friend"! It is quite another matter for God to call someone "His friend"!

God was shaping the man He would call "His friend." It is one thing to know and have God as "our Friend"! It is quite another matter for God to call someone "His friend"!

A friend is one who knows another so thoroughly that he is literally willing to "lay down one's life for his friends" (John 15:13).

In Abraham's entire life there is not even a hint of resistance to God or His will in his life. His heart for God was pure in its love and trust. A friend trusts! A friend responds to requests! A friend loves! A friend risks everything for another! A friend knows the Voice of his Lord! A friend is available and responsive! A friend never hesitates even when he does not know all the facts! It is enough that his friend has spoken!

When God is the One who calls you to Himself and offers a Covenant of love, there is no doubt, no hesitation, no rebellion, no fear, and no holding back of anything from Him.

Is there anything that you have held back from God? Take an inventory and ask God to search your heart. If He shows you something you have held back, write it down here. Then ask God to help you surrender it to Him.

____

____

____

Sin leads us to resist God, to even rebel against God.

But God knows what sin has done to our nature. Sin leads us to resist God, to even rebel against God. Sin leads to self-centeredness and self-interest. So God gave to Abraham His Presence to help him at every point of weakness or need. Since the heart was right in Abraham, he constantly appropriated God's resources. So God was revealed to him and through him to others. Abraham's family and friends and even his enemies knew God was with him and God was blessing him.

Above his own desires, his own inclinations, and his own reasoning, Abraham believed God, and God accounted (credited) that kind of life and trust for righteousness! God placed His righteousness over "His friend"

Abraham, and nothing then hindered Abraham from experiencing God's full capacity to bless him. The Scripture records that "the LORD had blessed Abraham in all things" (Gen. 24:1).

Further, in all God's relationship with Abraham He kept telling him what probably he could not grasp, but Abraham believed God when He said, "In you [and your seed] all the nations of the earth shall be blessed" (Gen. 12:3; 18:18; 22:18). God's eternal purpose was to invite Abraham to believe Him, love Him, and obey Him so He could, in the centuries to come, build a special people for Himself and through them bring the Messiah, the Savior. Through the Savior, His Own Son, God would provide eternal life to all who would obey Him (Heb. 5:7–10) and thus bless all the nations of the earth.

- **Review what God has shown you through the lesson today.**
- **Look back over your lesson and take time to underline or highlight key statements that God used to impact your life.**
- **Write a statement here that God used most in your life today:**

____

____

____

- **Turn to the end of the chapter and write your statement again. This will provide a weekly list of key statements for you to meditate on the last two days of the week.**

  ❑ CHECK THIS BOX AFTER YOU HAVE DONE SO.
- **Take time to pray, asking God to adjust your life to how He has spoken to you today.**
- **With whom do you need to share this truth today?**

____

SUMMARY STATEMENTS

- It is one thing to know and have God as "our Friend"! It is quite another matter for God to call someone "His friend"!
- Sin leads us to resist God, to even rebel against God.

DAY 2

An Heir of God

We have looked carefully at how God shapes the man He calls "His friend"! Now that we can see life as God sees it, each of us can be alert to and expectant of God working in us, and we can take our lives much more seriously. The Bible says that through *faith*—like Abraham—we, too, are heirs of the promises made to Abraham: "And if you are Christ's, then you are Abraham's seed, and heirs according to the promise" (Gal. 3:29).

What does it mean to be an heir? Paul declared confidently,

> *The Spirit Himself bears witness with our spirit that we are children of God, and if children, then heirs—heirs of God and joint heirs with Christ, if indeed we suffer with Him, that we may also be glorified together.*
>
> ROMANS 8:16–17

Do you know that you are now living your life as an heir of God and joint heir with Christ? How then should you live your life?

____

____

____

First, an heir is so by relationship. If one is a son, then one is an heir. All that is a part of the Father is now a vital part of the son. There is full access to the Father Himself. For instance, I respond to the voices of my children immediately. I respond to them differently from other children. I respond to my children's requests. They are my children.

My children can come in and go out of my home without knocking or asking. They belong to and live in my home. They can partake of what is in the cupboards and refrigerator. They can have the use of my car and my tools. Everything that is mine is theirs. How my children experience much of what is mine is limited only by their choice.

An heir also can carry and use my name. When my children tell others they are my children, people respond to them as to me. And for others to receive them is to receive me. They are treated according to their relationship to me.

Because of our relationship to Jesus Christ, we have access to the Father. So anxious is God that we know and receive and experience all that is ours as heirs of His, He has given us His Holy Spirit to make certain we do not neglect or lose or not know to appropriate what is ours in Jesus Christ. Jesus said,

> *However, when He, the Spirit of truth, has come, He will guide you into all truth; for He will not speak on His own authority, but whatever He hears He will speak; and He will tell you things to come. He will glorify Me, for He will take of what is Mine and declare it to you. All things that the Father has are Mine. Therefore I said that He will take of Mine and declare it to you.*
>
> JOHN 16:13–15

God has given us His Holy Spirit to make certain we do not neglect or lose or not know to appropriate what is ours in Jesus Christ.

All that is the Father's is Christ's. We are joint heirs with Him. The Holy Spirit hears all the Father wants us to know about being His children and immediately communicates it to us. We can then appropriate into our lives all He is and all He has to bless us with—just like Abraham.

The Holy Spirit hears all the Father wants us to know about being His children and immediately communicates it to us.

- **Review what God has shown you through the lesson today.**
- **Look back over your lesson and take time to underline or highlight key statements that God used to impact your life.**
- **Write a statement here that God used most in your life today:**

____

____

____

- **Turn to the end of the chapter and write your statement again. This will provide a weekly list of key statements for you to meditate on the last two days of the week.**

  ❏ CHECK THIS BOX AFTER YOU HAVE DONE SO.
- **Take time to pray, asking God to adjust your life to how He has spoken to you today.**
- **With whom do you need to share this truth today?**

____

SUMMARY STATEMENTS

- God has given us His Holy Spirit to make certain we do not neglect or lose or not know to appropriate what is ours in Jesus Christ.
- The Holy Spirit hears all the Father wants us to know about being His children and immediately communicates it to us.

DAY 3

A Friend of God

This is available to you—by *faith* and *obedience*! You, too, can be a "friend of God." And you, too, can be on mission with God so through you the nations of the earth can be blessed—not in exactly the same way but with Christ in a new way touch the nations of the world. It is a choice we make when God invites us into a Covenant relationship with Him through His Son.

It is a choice we make when God invites us into a Covenant relationship with Him through His Son.

The disciples heard just such a call from Jesus to "follow Me." They heard the call, not knowing where that would lead in their lives. In that relationship they were shaped carefully by Jesus for three and one-half years—at the Father's command. So they, too, entered into a relationship with God where their lives would touch the nations of the world, as Jesus gave them their Covenant invitation:

> *"Go therefore and make disciples of all the nations, baptizing them in the name of the Father and of the Son and of the Holy Spirit, teaching them to observe all things that I have commanded you; and lo, I am with you always, even to the end of the age."* Amen.
>
> MATTHEW 28:19–20

And He said to them,

> *Go into all the world and preach the gospel to every creature.*
>
> MARK 16:15

> *But you shall receive power when the Holy Spirit has come upon you; and you shall be witnesses to Me in Jerusalem, and in all Judea and Samaria, and to the end of the earth.*
>
> ACTS 1:8

How are you experiencing these truths in your life?

Can you say that you now receive Him fully in your everyday life?

How would friends know that you are now living your life as an heir of God and joint heir with Christ?

Do others say of you, as they said of Abraham, "God is with you in all that you do" (Gen. 21:22)? Why?

Is heaven (God) so pleased with your *faith* and *obedience* with Him that you can see clearly that He is saying to you, "Blessing I will bless you, and multiplying I will multiply your descendants"?

- Review what God has shown you through the lesson today.
- Look back over your lesson and take time to underline or highlight key statements that God used to impact your life.
- Write a statement here that God used most in your life today:

- Turn to the end of the chapter and write your statement again. This will provide a weekly list of key statements for you to meditate on the last two days of the week.

  ❑ CHECK THIS BOX AFTER YOU HAVE DONE SO.
- Take time to pray, asking God to adjust your life to how He has spoken to you today.
- Who do you need to share this truth with today?

Summary Statements

- It is a choice we make when God invites us into a Covenant relationship with Him through His Son.

DAY 4

Are You God's Friend?

You can be a "friend of God"! Jesus put it clearly to His disciples—and therefore to each of us:

You are My friends if you do whatever I command you.
John 15:14

Almost every word of this verse is filled with a Covenant Promise:

"You"—makes it so very personal. But the reality of this becoming real in your life lies with the same response in you as in Abraham—*faith* that brings immediate and thorough obedience. This is an obedience that enters a relationship with Him and that yields everything in your life to Him—now! It is a choice, clear and simple! Too many right now will say, "If He shows me when to go, I'll go!" God says, "Follow Me! I'll take you where I want you to go!" This fellowship comes after the commitment, as it did with Abraham. Right now, say to God, "I have heard Your Voice through Your Word in this study. I now say, 'Yes—Lord!'" Do it with all your heart and soul. "I know You will be shaping me, so You can use me. I am ready to respond. I choose this kind of Covenant of love with You—now!"

"My"—not just any relationship but a personal, real relationship with Him. Stop and remember who is speaking. It is God! Abraham knew this, and you and I must also. It is so personal, He assures you that He Himself is personally involved with you. Stand in awe of this!

"Friends"—the unsearchable riches in this word, when spoken by our Lord. Who can measure such an invitation from the mouth and Heart of our Lord? He knew ahead of time that if anyone became "His friend," he would receive everything He had in love to share. So He gave this word of invitation to His disciples, as His Father did to Abraham. Have you made this personal in your life? Do you hear in this verse your name? Have you said, "Yes, Lord! I would be Your friend"?

"If"—here is the heart of God's Covenant of love! "If" means there is a clear condition of response on our part. Here the response required is from the heart! Here stands the moment of truth. If He is God to me, the response will be, "Yes, Lord!" to every command He gives me! Only the heart will make this kind of a response to God at all times and whatever the cost. To say from the heart, at all times, "Not my will but Yours be done!" takes a special understanding of God and relationship to God. It may not be only in the big decisions, but in the little ones where the heart is revealed. When circumstances change (like a famine) and we must alter our plans, do we instinctively turn to God for counsel and do it completely? It may come in our finances, or in our choice of vocations, or when our health changes.

If He is God to me, the response will be, "Yes, Lord!" to every command He gives me!

If we are servants of Christ, we will seek and obey His will alone. "If" we respond to Him, then we are "His friends." If we do not, we still have a ways to go in our relationship.

If we are servants of Christ, we will seek and obey His will alone. "If" we respond to Him, then we are "His friends." If we do not, we still have a ways to go in our relationship.

"You do"—it is not the one who says "Lord, Lord" who enters the kingdom of heaven. That is, who shares in the full experience of God's rule and reign in life, like Abraham, who saw God Sovereignly work in Egypt and in the battle with the kings. Only the one "who does the will of My Father in heaven" (Matt. 7:21) experiences God working Sovereignly in and around his life and family. Faith, without works, is dead. For Abraham to say he believes God and not gather in his family and move to where God would show him is not *faith* at all. It is rebellion and disbelief. A "friend of God" would never fail to obey Him when He spoke in a command to him.

A "friend of God" would never fail to obey Him when He spoke in a command to him.

If this element was the only standard God gave, doing what He commanded, would He consider you "His friend" by the way you have been responding to Him in your life?

"Whatever"—the servant does not tell the master what he will or will not do. The servant says an immediate, "Yes, Lord!" A friend does not hesitate regardless of the request, even if it costs his life. John put it this way: "By this we know love, because He laid down His life for us" (1 John 3:16).

In another place John recorded Jesus describing His relationship to His disciples as a "good shepherd": "I am the good shepherd. The good shepherd gives His life for the sheep" (John 10:11).

God's required "whatever" with Abraham was for him to lay down the life of his son. And this he did freely! A friend of God responds completely—whatever is asked.

Have you placed limitations on your love to God? Do you have some areas of your life that are "out of bounds" for God to touch? Is there definitely no "whatever You ask" in your relationship with your Lord? If so then Jesus says you are not "His friend." He may faithfully be your Friend, but you are not "His friend"! No exceptions!

What has God done in your life, and how have you responded so that God can call you "His friend"?

- **Review what God has shown you through the lesson today.**
- **Look back over your lesson and take time to underline or highlight key statements that God used to impact your life.**
- **Write a statement here that God used most in your life today:**

- **Turn to the end of the chapter and write your statement again. This will provide a weekly list of key statements for you to meditate on the last two days of the week.**

  ❑ CHECK THIS BOX AFTER YOU HAVE DONE SO.
- **Take time to pray, asking God to adjust your life to how He has spoken to you today.**
- **With whom do you need to share this truth today?**

Summary Statements

- If He is God to me, the response will be, "Yes, Lord!" to every command He gives me!
- If we are servants of Christ, we will seek and obey His will alone. "If" we respond to Him, then we are "His friends." If we do not, we still have a ways to go in our relationship.
- A "friend of God" would never fail to obey Him when He spoke in a command to him.

DAY 5

Are You God's Friend? (Continued)

Jesus put this truth very clearly in another way when He told His disciples:

> *He who has My commandments and keeps them, it is he who loves Me. And he who loves Me will be loved by My Father, and I will love him and manifest Myself to him . . . He who does not love Me does not keep My words; and the word which you hear is not Mine but the Father's who sent Me.*
>
> **John 14:21, 24**

Does this not clearly confirm that the only kind of love relationship that God is looking for and that is acceptable to Him is a life that obeys? But He also leaves no doubt whatsoever about the person who does not obey!

Jesus followed this up by connecting a heart and life that love and obey with the Father's love and measureless Blessing. He said,

> *And in that day you will ask Me nothing. Most assuredly, I say to you, whatever you ask the Father in My name He will give you. Until now you have asked nothing in My name. Ask, and you will receive, that your joy may be full . . . For the Father Himself loves you, because you have loved Me, and have believed that I came forth from God.*
>
> **John 16:23–24, 27**

Jesus said, "Whatever you ask the Father . . . will give you . . . for the Father Himself loves you." This is what Abraham came to know so completely. This is what the disciples came to experience in their lives. And this is God's open invitation to all His children, "If . . ."

Because He is God, He never makes "suggestions"—only commands!

"I command you"—because He is God, He never makes "suggestions"—only commands! He is perfect love by nature, so He never speaks except from perfect love. Perfect love knows what is best and His commands are always best! Perfect love will withhold from us that for which we are not ready or able to receive (John 16:12). But "no good thing will He withhold from those who walk uprightly" (Ps. 84:11).

Perfect knowledge will always command what is right! So every command from God is right, and the one who knows how to be this way will always obey.

Perfect knowledge will always command what is right! So every command from God is right, and the one who knows how to be this way will always obey. This is how you can know a "friend of God." He always does what his Lord commands!

Are you, by this standard, a "friend of God"? You can be! It is a choice! But it is a choice of the heart that loves Him with all the heart, soul, mind, and strength, and obeys what He commands—immediately, thoroughly, and with great *faith:* "'Abraham believed God, and it was accounted to him for righteousness.' And he was called the friend of God" (James 2:23). And you can, too. His invitation is open. Choose Him and choose life!

> *I call heaven and earth as witnesses today against you, that I have set before you life and death, blessing and cursing; therefore choose life, that both you and your descendants may live; that you may love the* LORD *your God, that you may obey His voice, and that you may cling to Him, for He is your life and the length of your days; and that you may dwell in the land which the* LORD *swore to your fathers, to Abraham, Isaac, and Jacob, to give them.*
>
> DEUTERONOMY 30:19–20

GOD'S ENCOUNTERS WITH ABRAHAM

Remember this chart in the Introduction? Take time to draw your own chart. Remember to place the high, mid, and low points on the chart. This will become your testimoney of God's encounters with your life!

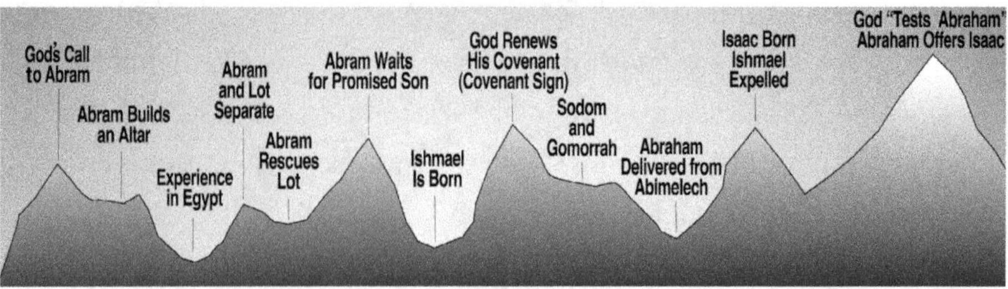

In what areas of your life do you need to ask God's help to learn obedience? Will you commit your life right now to be known as a "friend of God"?

- Review what God has shown you through the lesson today.
- Look back over your lesson and take time to underline or highlight key statements that God used to impact your life.
- Write a statement here that God used most in your life today:

- Turn to the end of the chapter and write your statement again. This will provide a weekly list of key statements for you to meditate on the last two days of the week.

  ❑ CHECK THIS BOX AFTER YOU HAVE DONE SO.
- Take time to pray, asking God to adjust your life to how He has spoken to you today.
- With whom do you need to share this truth today?

SUMMARY STATEMENTS

- Because He is God, He never makes "suggestions"—only commands!
- Perfect knowledge will always command what is right! So every command from God is right, and the one who knows how to be this way will always obey.

KEY STATEMENTS FOR MEDITATION

Day 1

Day 2

Day 3

Day 4

Day 5

Appendix

It is always helpful to secure "the bigger picture"! A handy chart that connects Abraham's age with the activity of God is useful. But in connecting the events in Abraham's life with God's revealing Himself and God's developing character qualities in his life, it is vital! God develops character in and through real-life experiences. The accumulation of character qualities develops ultimately into a "man God calls His friend"!

Seeing Abraham's life from God's activities and perspective may help you reexamine your character. And seeing how God does not stop us from making mistakes, but does redeem us out of them will help you know how to respond to God in your failures and sin. But even more helpful is the opportunity to see ahead of time, through Abraham's life, the ways of God so that you may respond faithfully, immediately, and thoroughly to God as you live out your life with Him.

Several of the age dates listed are my own observation. The nature of God revealed and the character qualities developed are my own observations taken from Scripture. You may see much more than I have seen. The key is that you do make the connection between God's revealing Himself and the character development in Abraham. The more God reveals Himself, the more Abraham can trust Him. The more Abraham knows God in life experiences, the deeper his *faith*.

God had a mighty purpose in developing Abraham as "His friend." He does for your life, too!

HOW GOD DEVELOPS THE		
ABRAHAM'S AGE	SCRIPTURE	ABRAHAM'S LIFE (Events in His Life)
60 (?)	Acts 7:2–4 Genesis 15:7 Genesis 11:27–32	God's Call to Abram—Ur
75	Genesis 12:1–4	God's Call to Abram—Hara
	Genesis 12:7–8	Abram Builds an Altar
	Genesis 12:10–20	Experience in Egypt
	Genesis 13:1–18	Abram and Lot Separate
	Genesis 14:1–16	Abram Rescues Lot
	Genesis 14:17–24	Melchizedek
	Genesis 15:1–21	Abram Waits for Promised Son—Covenant Renewal
86	Genesis 16:1–16	Ishmael Is Born
	Genesis 17:1–27	God Renews His Covenant (Covenant Sign)
	Genesis 18:1–19:38	Sodom and Gomorrah
	Genesis 20:1–18	Abraham Delivered from Abimelech
100	Genesis 21:1–21	Isaac Born Ishmael Expelled
100+	Genesis 21:22–34	Covenant with Abimelech
115	Genesis 22:1–24	God "Tests Abraham" Abraham Offers Isaac
137	Genesis 23:1–20	Sarah Dies Chooses Burial Plot for Sara
140 (?)	Genesis 24:1–67	A Bride Provided for Isaac
175	Genesis 25:1–18	Death of Abraham Isaac Is the Heir

AN HE CALLS "HIS FRIEND"

)D REVEALS HIMSELF	ABRAHAM'S RESPONSE (Character Qualities Developed)
od Who Chooses	Trust
od Who Calls/Promises	Obedience
od Who Is Worshiped	Worshiper
od Who Protects	Fear of God
od Who Guides	Peacemaker
od Is His Shield	Strength in Leadership
Am Your Exceedingly eat Reward	Integrity
od Who Is Faithful	Faith
od Who Sees and Hears	Consistency
Am Almighty od Who Honors Character	Blamelessness
od of Mercy/Judgment	Intercessor
od Who Intervenes od Who Makes Prophets	Godly Sensitivity
od Has His "Fullness of me" God Who Separates	Focused Patience
od Is With You	Steadfastness
od Who "Tests" od Is Provider ovenant-Keeping God	Faithfulness
od Who Comforts od Who Knows the Future	Thankfulness Hope
od Fulfills Covenant to scendants	Descendants
od Is Changeless od Is Faithful od Is Sufficient	Trust/Perseverance

Notes

Introduction

1. It is seen in almost all others greatly used of God, but is clear in Abraham's life.

Unit 2

1. Henry T. Blackaby and Claude V. King, *Experiencing God: Knowing and Doing the Will of God* (Nashville: LifeWay Press, 1998).

Unit 4

1. You will notice that I am using New Testament Scriptures on purpose, to show that what God was doing in and with Abram is what you see in its fulfillment in Christ. This connection is crucial to see the larger purposes of God.
2. Several books have been written describing this touch of God, one being *Flames of Freedom* by Irwin Lutzer.

Unit 5

1. Note carefully how Jesus prayed that His disciples' faith would not "utterly fail" when they were tested (Luke 22:31–32).
2. All through the Old Testament, God warns His people not to "go down to Egypt" for help, but to turn to Him for help (e.g., Isa. 30–31).

Unit 7

1. See Genesis 16:16 to notice he was eighty-six years old when Ishmael was born.
2. The descendants of her son, Ishmael, have become the Arabs.

Unit 11

1. I wrote a study on this with Richard Blackaby called *When God Speaks* (Nashville: LifeWay Press, 1995) and a course on this kind of a relationship with God, *Experiencing God: Knowing and Doing the Will of God* (Nashville: LifeWay Press).

About the Authors

HENRY T. BLACKABY HAS SPENT HIS LIFE IN MINISTRY. He has served as a music director, Christian education director, and senior pastor in churches in California and Canada; his first church assignment was in 1958. During his local church ministry, Dr. Blackaby became a college president, a missionary, and later an executive in Southern Baptist Convention life.

Dr. Blackaby formerly served on staff at the North American Mission Board in Alpharetta, Georgia, as Special Assistant to the President. Through the office of Revival and Spiritual Awakening of the Southern Baptist Convention, he provided leadership to thousands of pastors and laymen across North America. He also served concurrently as Special Assistant to the Presidents of the International Mission Board and LifeWay Christian Resources for global revival.

In the early 90's Henry Blackaby became one of North America's best-selling Christian authors, committing the rest of his life to helping people know and experience God.

The author of over a dozen books, Dr. Blackaby is a graduate of the University of British Columbia, Vancouver, Canada. He has completed his Th.M. degree from Golden Gate Baptist Theological Seminary. He has also received four honorary doctorate degrees.

Henry Blackaby and his wife, Marilynn, have five married children, all serving in Christian ministry. They are also blessed with thirteen grandchildren. Henry is now serving as the president of Henry Blackaby Ministries.

KERRY L. SKINNER HAS SERVED MORE THAN TWENTY-FIVE YEARS as a pastor and Christian educator focusing on personal discipleship. A graduate of Campbellsville College and Southwestern Baptist Theological Seminary, he has authored or co-authored many books with Dr. Henry Blackaby and Dr. Henry Brandt, including *Marriage God's Way*, *The Power of the Call*, and *Chosen to Be God's Prophet*. After nine years of assisting Dr. Blackaby in the development and writing of discipleship curriculum, Skinner currently serves as the Teaching Pastor of First Baptist Church of West Palm Beach, Florida. He and his wife, Elaine, have one son and two grandchildren.

HENRY BLACKABY MINISTRIES

Henry Blackaby Ministries exists to help people experience a life-changing relationship with God that dynamically affects their home, church, and business through a message of revival and spiritual awakening.

They seek to help people experience God through preaching, teaching, conference speaking, leadership training, the production and presentation of ministry materials, and various media outlets, including radio and the Internet.

For further information about Henry Blackaby Ministries, please contact:

Henry Blackaby Ministries
P.O. Box 161228
Atlanta, GA 30321
hbm@henryblackaby.com
www.henryblackaby.com

Printed in the USA
CPSIA information can be obtained
at www.ICGtesting.com
JSHW051914200524
63433JS00003B/6